Cloud of Witnesses

✠

Cloud of Witnesses

The Floyd-Lewis Chronicles: the Growth of Catholicism and its Impact Beyond the Appalachian Region

Father Harry E. Winter, O.M.I.

Editing, design, and layout by Saving Stories.
www.saving-stories.com

ISBN: 978-0-9910772-1-2

Cover photographs:
Portrait of Governor John Floyd Jr. courtesy of the Library of Virginia.
Photograph of Lynnside mansion by Jim Glanville, 2014.

Dedication

This book is dedicated to Dr. James Glanville, Ph.D., and to Mrs. Lynn (née Keiley) Spellman, each of whom contributed without reserve to this story.

Dr. James Glanville (1941-2019) had extensively researched the impact of Virginia west of the Blue Ridge Mountains. His wife, Deena Flinchum, maintains the website holstonia.net that contains his many writings and lectures.

Mrs. Lynn Spellman (1943-2016) was the last direct descendant of Governor Floyd to farm the estate in Sweet Springs, West Virginia. Her website lynnside.org had been taken over and expanded by Glanville.

It was my privilege to be Lynn's pastor from 1982 to 1991, and to remain close to her until her death. It was also my privilege to introduce Jim to Lynn, and watch their friendship develop. I am truly blessed to include both of them in my own Cloud of Witnesses (Heb. 12:1).

Acknowledgments

This history was originally written as an article for the journal *U.S. Catholic Historian* volume 38(1) Winter 2020. That volume focused on articles concerning Ante-Bellum Catholicism, meaning Catholicism in the United States between the Revolutionary War and the Civil War. Being much too long for the journal, the editor, Fr. David Endres, expressed a hope that it would find a publisher elsewhere. I appreciate his encouragement very much.

My gratitude to David Arthur, our retired Administrator at the Immaculate Heart of Mary Residence in Tewksbury, Massachusetts. He did much of the formatting when this article was in its original form. He was helped by his Administrative Assistant, Alice Chin. Both showed admirable patience.

It was Fr. Patrick Healy, O.M.I., who recommended Saving Stories to me, from his excellent experience with their work in publishing his two books, *The Finger of God* (2015) and *Vietnam Vignettes* (2020). Thus it was that I discovered their editor, Ms. Chris Wisniewski, who assisted with editing, changed the pesky footnotes to endnotes, and helped so much with the photos and the design of this book.

Contents

Preface

John Floyd Jr. (1783-1837) was the last governor of Virginia under its pre-Revolutionary War constitution, and the first under the post-war constitution (1830-1834). During his six terms in United States Congress from 1817 to 1829, he became well known for promoting the Oregon Territory. His first cousin Charles Floyd was the only member of the Lewis and Clark Expedition to die during the course of the expedition. Charles died on August 20, 1804, on a bluff of the Missouri River near present day Sioux City, Iowa, probably of a burst appendix. The Floyd family and its descendants are very much aware of the family's influence in the United States from Oregon through the entire Midwest and the South. After an initially good relationship with President Andrew Jackson, John Floyd Jr.'s relationship with Jackson turned stormy.

John Floyd Jr. married Letitia Preston Floyd (1779-1852), and together they had twelve children. Their eldest daughter, Letitia Floyd, married William Lynn Lewis, and they eventually settled in Sweet Springs, West Virginia. John Floyd and his wife visited them there every summer at their home "Lynnside." It was there that John Floyd Jr. died on August 16, 1837. He is buried in the historic Lewis Family Cemetery on the knoll behind the Lewis home, Lynnside.

The governor's wife, Letitia Preston Floyd, was also the sister of a governor of Virginia, James Patton Preston, as well as the mother of a governor of Virginia, John Buchanan Floyd. Letitia's spirited correspondence with the first Catholic bishop of West Virginia, Most Rev. Richard Whelan (Bishop of Richmond, Virginia, from 1841 to 1850 and of Wheeling, West Virginia, from 1850 to 1874), and her conversion to Catholicism were recently explored by Jim Glanville in *The Smithfield Review,* volumes 19 and 20. Glanville's sudden death on November 22, 2019, deprived us of our only link to the owner of the Lewis Family Cemetery where John and Letitia Floyd and their Lewis descendants are buried. Fortunately, Glanville's widow, Deena Flinchum, of Blacksburg, Virginia, has arranged for the preservation of Glanville's two websites: lynnside.org that gives much material on Sweet Springs, and holstonia.net that contains Glanville's many other writings.

The New Testament includes the Letter to the Hebrews, with its very interesting expression that every person is surrounded by a "Cloud of Witnesses" (Heb. 12:1). The author is encouraging his readers who were discouraged by persecution and disasters to persevere joyfully.

When Pope Francis spoke to a joint session of the United States Congress on September 24, 2015, he proposed four Americans as part of our Cloud of Witnesses, although he did not use that term. Of the four, two are not formally Roman Catholic, Abraham Lincoln and Martin Luther King Jr., and the two who are formally Roman Catholic, are very different from each other, Dorothy Day and Thomas Merton.

Let us remember that President John Adam's wife, Abigail, wrote to her husband on March 31, 1776, during the debate over the Declaration of Independence saying, "Remember the ladies" in the discussion concerning the place of women in the new nation. I hope you will see that Governor Floyd's wife, Letitia Preston Floyd, was a Pioneer Catholic American Feminist rivaling Abigail Adams.

I have driven the 20 miles from the rectory in Union, West Virginia, to Sweet Springs over 500 times. The section from Gap Mills to Sweet Springs is one of the most beautiful places in the world. After reading this account, you may want to visit Sweet Springs either in person, or at least virtually through online photographs.

The text in this book is personal, the endnotes were added so that historians can begin to do the extensive work needed to better understand the historic significance of the Floyd family. It is my hope that in reading this account of Governor John Floyd Jr., his wife, Letitia Preston Floyd, and the seven of their children who survived into adulthood that you will enlarge your own Cloud of Witnesses to help you in your own life.

Portrait of Governor John Floyd Jr.
courtesy of the Library of Virginia.

Painting by William Garl Browne. It was given to the Library of Virginia in 1873 by John B. Floyd's widow, along with a painting of Governor John B. Floyd by the same artist.

— CHAPTER ONE —

John Floyd Jr. (1783–1837), towards Appalachian Catholicism

John Floyd Jr. was born on April 24, 1783, at Floyd's Station, Virginia (now Jefferson County, Kentucky). His father, John Floyd, was killed by Native Americans twelve days before his son's birth. His mother was Sallie Jane Buchanan. Charles H. Ambler, who edited Floyd's journal, observes that Floyd's grandfather William Floyd was both a frontiersman and a Tidewater gentleman.[1]

Ambler's book, while a good resource, is very short, indicating that a full study of John Floyd is still to be written, and a modern biography of him is needed.

James Glanville underlines that the Colony of Virginia, which in 1734 included Orange County, extended to the east bank of the Mississippi River where the modern cities of St. Paul and Minneapolis, Minnesota, are today.[2] So the young Floyd would have heard of his family's explorations, and would have been quite aware of Virginia's influence on the growth of the country.

Some authorities state that Floyd was of Native American ancestry, and the U.S. Congress listed him first in that category stating that he was a "Representative of Native Proven indisputable ancestry." However a Native American who once touched Floyd's hair felt he was of African-American descent. [3]

R.A. Brock writing in 1888 states, "The tradition in the Floyd family is that he [John Floyd Sr.] married a half-breed Indian girl. This, if true, would account in some measure for the striking physique of the Colonels John Floyd, father and son." Later Brock added, "Governor Floyd was of a singularly handsome and commanding physique. 'In height and erectness of person, gait, color and straightness of hair, swarthy skin, and, above all, his keen and dark rolling eye, he was the personification of an Indian chief.'"[4]

Perhaps Ambler's viewpoint shows two things: he was not a disinterested author, and his insight is true. "Of the many wonderful families of Virginia there are few to be found anywhere more interesting and important than that of John Floyd and his wife, Letitia."[5]

As a youth, John Floyd Jr. experienced poverty due to the mismanagement of funds by his stepfather. That and poor health made him withdraw from Dickinson College in Carlisle, Pennsylvania, where he had enrolled at the age of thirteen, in 1796. It was there that he became a member of the Union Philosophical Society.

After his stepfather died in 1801, Floyd moved to Philadelphia. There Dr. Benjamin Rush (1746-1813) became his medical school instructor, and later his wife's doctor.[6] After an apprenticeship in Kentucky, Floyd married Letitia Preston in 1804. He then returned to enroll in the University of Pennsylvania Medical School where Rush was the leading professor.

Floyd was a surgeon with the rank of major in the Virginia State Militia from 1807 to 1812. He then served in the Virginia House of Delegates from 1812 to 1817, and during that time he was considered "a strong nationalist."[7] In 1817, he was elected to the U.S. House of Representatives, where he served from March 4, 1817, to March 3, 1829.

Floyd brought his second and fourth surviving sons, William Preston Floyd (born Jan. 16, 1809) and Benjamin Rush Floyd (born Dec. 10, 1811), with him to Washington, D.C. He enrolled them in what Glanville describes as "a Catholic school for secondary education that was associated with Georgetown Academy."[8]

Why did Floyd choose a Catholic school for his sons? Ambler notes that another John Floyd in England, who was an ancestor of Floyd's and a veteran of the Spanish Armada "was knighted by Queen Elizabeth, and later became a writer of some note and a lecturer in the Society of Jesus."[9] Unfortunately for us, being a "lecturer in the Society of Jesus" (perhaps he was referring to the Jesuits) is a very enigmatic reference.

Although Congressman Floyd enrolled his sons in Georgetown Prep, they did not immediately join the Catholic Church. However the seed of Catholicism for the entire family was probably planted there. That is confirmed by Glanville's discovery of a writer known only as "JMJ," who in 1887 "suggests that the origin of the engagement of the Floyd family with Catholicism occurred when Congressman John Floyd sent two of his young sons to Georgetown related schools in Washington city."[10]

John Floyd Jr. was elected governor of Virginia in 1830. In that office, he pushed for the abolition of slavery in Virginia. He felt he had the votes, but the Nat Turner Rebellion on August 1831 destroyed that effort.[11] Glanville concludes that Floyd believed that "slavery was a wasteful, inefficient labor system."[12] Floyd wrote in his journal on December 26, 1831, "I shall not rest until slavery is abolished in Virginia."[13]

Glanville documents that this did not prevent Floyd from owning slaves himself. The 1810 census notes that he owned four "unspecified." The census shows him owning five males in 1820, and thirteen males in 1830, but none in 1840.[14]

Following Nat Turner's rebellion in 1831, Floyd became known as "the apostle of secession." The response of some of the northern abolitionists to the rebellion convinced the governor, and many others in Virginia, that interference from outside Virginia was repulsive.[15] In this matter, Floyd shared the convictions of Richard Vincent Whelan, the Catholic bishop of Wheeling, who was also very much against slavery, yet was equally against abolitionist interference.[16]

In the 1832 presidential election, Floyd received South Carolina's eleven electoral votes, demonstrating his influence throughout the south.

It was during his time as governor that we have the most documentation of Floyd's attitude towards the Catholic Church and other churches. On April 3, 1831, he "went to old Baptist Church to hear Mr. Broadus preach." Apparently, the preaching did not live up to what he had been told he would hear. He noted on May 16, 1831, that he "went to the Catholic Chapel today to hear the eloquent Mr. Shriber, a Jesuit Priest. He was ill and could not preach."[17] On June 5, he wrote:

> Much preaching through the city today and has been for some time. It is fortunate that the Constitution permits everybody to preach and pray as they please else this fanaticism which has seized upon the minds of the people, or new zeal, or as they call it a "revival of religion" would seek to satisfy itself by the shedding the blood of their fellow citizens "for love of the Lord they adore" as was done so often in England and most of the governments on the continent of Europe.[18]

On November 20, 1831, Floyd simply wrote, "went to the Catholic Church." On May 27, 1832, he "went to the chapel to hear Mr. O'Brien, who is a man of talents and a respectable orator."[19]

On November 17, 1832, when he heard of the death of "Charles Carroll of Maryland, the last signer of the Declaration of Independence," he reflected, "He was a Catholic by persuasion, a pious, good man. I am fearful the liberty of the country, the Declaration of whose Independence he signed, will not long outlive the last of its signers."[20]

While he was governor, Floyd maintained a pew at St. Peter's, the cathedral of Richmond. It is here that his daughters first showed signs of joining the Catholic Church. Glanville notes that the baptismal records do not give the exact dates, but Fr. Joseph Magri records that Floyd's eldest daughter, also named Letitia, was baptized "about 1832," and that it "caused a sensation throughout the state."[21] After Floyd's daughter Letitia chose the Catholic Church, she was followed by her two surviving sisters and three of her four surviving brothers.

On May 30, 1832, Floyd wrote in his journal a moving remembrance stating that it was the 28th anniversary of his wedding to Letitia Preston. He reminded himself fondly that they have

Lynnside mansion, Sweet Springs, West Virginia, 2014

"now living and grown, except three, nine children, four sons and five daughters, finer children no parents ever had, both for size, talents, morals, beauty and good tempers. Their education has been of the best."[22] Floyd's wife was the leading reason for their children's remarkable education.

Floyd had never enjoyed good health. A stroke during his last year as governor almost killed him, but he recovered enough to serve out his term.

By then his eldest daughter, Letitia, had married William Lynn Lewis, and they had settled in Sweet Springs, West Virginia. John Floyd and his wife visited them there every summer at their home "Lynnside." Floyd and his family were visiting with his daughter at Lynnside in mid-August of 1837 when he fell mortally ill.

Fifty years later, when I first visited the Lynnside home in the autumn of 1982, Lynn Spellman, the last descendant of Letitia Floyd Lewis to farm the estate, told me that when Floyd fell sick the family had felt he might have a contagious disease such as diphtheria or cholera. Therefore, they moved him from the manor to a nearby root cellar where he died sometime between August 16 to August 21, 1837. The exact day is uncertain.[23]

It is possible Floyd was received into the Catholic Church on his deathbed in the root cellar. Fr. Joseph Magri, in *The Catholic Encyclopedia* of 1912, asserts Floyd became Catholic without giving any details. However there was never any documentation, so the Diocese of Richmond disputes his reception into the Catholic Church.[24] Even if John Floyd Jr. never formally joined the Catholic Church himself, he did begin the process for his children to become Catholic by enrolling two of his four sons in a Catholic school and allowing his daughters to become Catholics in their teens.

The eulogy for Floyd given at a Memorial Service in Richmond on August 27, 1837, concentrated on "a man gifted with the noblest qualities of our nature; scrupulously just, and even obstinately honest.... None who knew Governor Floyd well could have failed to receive the impression that nature had endued him with the qualities of a hero."[25]

Surprisingly, the grave of this respected man was left unmarked until about 1930 when Miss Coralie Lewis, the last family member to live in the Lynnside mansion, had a marker erected.[26]

CHAPTER ONE ENDNOTES

1. Charles H. Ambler, *Life and Diary of John Floyd* (Richmond: Richmond Press, 1918), 11-12; online at lynnside.org, table of contents. Ambler's book is also at archive.org / stream / lifediaryofjohnf00am

2. Jim Glanville, "Virginia's Western Counties and the Making of America," *Journal of the Historical Society of Western Virginia*, 22 (2016-2017) 12. Also available on holstonia.net.

3. "List of Native Americans in the U.S. Congress," *Wikipedia*; geni.com / projects / Native-American-Tribes-State-of-West-Virgina / people / 9819. Ambler explains at length the "family tradition of uncertain origin," 11-12. Austin Floyd recently discovered the African-American possibility in the collection "Documents and correspondence pertaining to the life and genealogy of Colonel George Rogers Clark Floyd: Complied by Colonel Robert L. Floyd" at West Virginia University in a letter dated 26 June 1951, from Elizabeth S. Francis from 1027 Westover Avenue, Norfolk, 7, Virginia to Colonel Robert L. Floyd, Hon-Ret, 2054 Lincoln Ave., Chicago 14, Ill.

4. R.A. (Robert Alonzo) Brock, *Virginia and Virginians* (Hardesty: Virginia, 1888) 158, 162, with no source of quote on 162.

5. Ambler, *Life*, 81.

6. For the recent revival in Rush's reputation, see Stephen Fried, *Benjamin Rush: Revolution, Madness & The Visionary Doctor Who Became a Founding Father* (New York: Crown, 2018). Melissa Block interview Fried on PBS radio on September 2, 2018, and the University of Pennsylvania *Gazette* editor John Prendergast published "Rush on the Mind," excerpted from the book, 117 (Nov / Dec 2018) 48-53, 55-56, interview "Rush Revealed," 53-55.

7. Ambler, *Life*, 34; en.wikipedia.org / wiki / John-Floyd-(Virginian—politician).

8. Glanville, "Governor John Floyd, Letitia Preston Floyd, and the Catholic Church," *The Smithfield Review (SR)* 19 (2015):124. For an interesting view of the Catholic Georgetown schools from the perspective of the debate over Brett Kavanaugh's appointment to the U.S. Supreme Court see Patrick Coyle, "Georgetown Prep after the Smear," nationalreview.com / 2018 / 10 / georgetown-prep-kavanaugh-confirmation-media-circus-damage.

9. Ambler, *Life*, 10.

10. Glanville, *SR* 19:124.

11. Also called the "Southhampton Insurrection," Brock, *Virginia and Virginians*, 160-61.

12. Jim Glanville and Ryan Mays, "A Sketch of Letitia Preston Floyd and Some of Her Letters," *SR* 19:96. He is also intrigued that Floyd kept slaves.

13. Ambler, *Life*, 172; 88-92; 96-97.

14. Jim Glanville and Ryan Mays, "Letitia Preston Floyd: Supplementary Notes," *SR* 20 (2016) 73; also *SR* 19 (2015) 144, n. 8.

15. Ambler, *Life*, 161-68; Glanville, *SR* 19, 95.

16. See James H. Bailey, *A History of the Diocese of Richmond, The Formative Years* (Richmond: Chancery Office, 1956), 100; John Loughery, *Dagger John, Archbishop Hughes and the Making of Irish America* (Ithaca: Cornell University Press, 2018) 2-3, 297.

17. Ambler, *Life*, 135, 144.

18. Ibid, 145-46.

19. Ibid, 170, 193.

20. Ibid, 200.

21. Glanville, *SR* 19:123. *Bailey, A History*, is the source for Floyd renting a pew (65-66), but he mixes up John Floyd, John Floyd Jr. and John Buchanan Floyd (66).

22. Ambler, *Life*, 189.

23. August 16 date: geni.com/people/John-Floyd-5th U-S-Governor of Virginia: "The Preston Family Bible preserved in the Library of Virginia: August 16, 1837 at sunrise on Thursday at the Sweet Springs in Virginia:" (Richmond: Richmond Press, 1918); Ambler, August 16, *Life*, 118. August 17 date: *Wikipedia*. August 21 date: concrete grave slab installed in the 1930s by Miss Coralie Lewis, the last family member to live in the mansion of Lynnside.

24. Fr. Joseph Magri, "Virginia," *The Catholic Encyclopedia* (New York: Robert Appleton Company, 1912) 15: Online at newadvent.org/cathen/15451a.htm. On January 22, 2019, I received a folder from Richmond Catholic Diocesan Archivist Edie Jeter of seven letters recently discovered in the Chancellor's Office research files, 1950–1965, Bishop Russell, dealing with *The Catholic Encyclopedia* conversion report. These letters are dated from November 28, 1953, to December 17, 1953, and come to the same conclusion: no proof for the encyclopedia statement has yet been found. Harry E. Winter, *St. John's Catholic Chapel, Sweet Springs, West Virginia, A Brief History* (White Sulphur Springs, West Virginia: Knights of Columbus, 1999): 2. This booklet is based on the Rededication Mass booklet of April 17, 1983:4. Online at lynnside.org. More than 1,000 printed copies have been distributed between the 1983 Mass and the August 15, 2018 Mass.

25. John Hampden Pleasants, obituary for John Floyd Jr., Richmond *Whig*, August 24, 1837, quoted in Brock, *Virginia and Virginians*, 162.

26. Ibid, 118.

— CHAPTER TWO —

Letitia Preston Floyd (1779-1852), Pioneer Catholic Feminist

Glanville thoroughly explored the life and writings of Letitia Preston Floyd, and he found some previously unknown writings. He concludes that she was "a remarkable woman whom history has badly neglected.... Surprisingly, despite many efforts to find one, there is no known picture of her."[1]

Letitia was born on September 29, 1779, at Smithfield Plantation, Virginia, which her parents, William and Susanna Smith Preston, owned. Today the restored Smithfield Plantation House in Blacksburg, Virginia, is an important historical resource. Glanville had found the staff to be most helpful, as I had earlier.[2]

James Patton (1692-1675), an uncle of Letitia Preston Floyd's, had been killed by Shawnee Indians in the Draper's Meadow Massacre of July, 1775. Letitia revered Mary Draper Ingles, a young girl who escaped from captivity following the massacre, traveling more than eight hundred miles to return home.[3]

William and Susanna Preston gave their children excellent tutors, as Letitia makes clear in her "Dear Rush" letter below. Letitia travelled to Kentucky at the age of 24 to visit her older sister. There she met John Floyd Jr., who had just turned 20. She fell deeply in love with Floyd,[4] and they married in 1804.

John and Letitia's first child, Susanna Smith Floyd, was born at Smithfield on March 14, 1805. She died on August 29, 1806. A son, John Buchanan Floyd, was born at Smithfield on June 1, 1806. Glanville reports that the Floyd's next residence is known only from the birthplace of their son George Rogers Clark Floyd, whose birth was listed in Montgomery County. The records of the Daughters of the American Revolution (DAR) list his birthplace as "the home of Mrs. Eliza Madison in Roanoke, Virginia."[5]

Another son, William Preston Floyd, was born in Christiansburg, Virginia, on January 15, 1809. Here the DAR records differ significantly from Glanville, with George Rogers Clark Floyd also being listed as born on January 15, 1809. Nowhere are they listed as twins. George died on August 15, 1808. According to Glanville, a second son given the same name—George Rogers Clarke Floyd—was born at Smithfield in September of 1810. His birth is listed as January 15, 1809 according to the DAR. Benjamin Rush Floyd was the final child to be born at Smithfield on December 10, 1811.

Their daughter Letitia Preston Floyd was born "at or near Blacksburg" on June 6, 1814, according to the DAR, and in March of 1814 near Blacksburg according to Glanville.[6] Glanville believes at that time the family was in the process of moving from Smithfield to Thorn Spring Plantation near the town of Pulaski, Virginia, about 20 miles south of Blackburg. Another daughter, Eliza Lavalette Floyd, was born at Thorn Spring on December 16, 1816, and Nicketti Buchanan Floyd was born on June 6, 1819. Coraly Patton Floyd's birth was on January 26, 1882 [sic, this date is impossible, but was listed by the DAR]. She died on July 14, 1833. Thomas Lewis Preston Floyd was born on August 16, 1824. He died on September 4, 1824. Finally, Mary Lewis Mourning Floyd was born on March 18, 1827. She died on July 26, 1833. Glanville states that Coraly and Mary both died of scarlet fever.[7]

Thorn Spring was a legacy from Letitia's father. It became their cherished home from the latter part of 1814 until John's death in August of 1837.[8] During Floyd's twelve years as a Congressman in Washington from 1817 to 1829 and his four years as governor in Richmond from 1830 to 1834 Thorn Spring was his refuge, where his wife was his confidante and advisor.

Glanville almost literally excavated the Thorn Spring site. He visited it himself in March of 2014. He then obtained permission from the current owner, Mr. Sam Gregory, to take April Martin, a consultant with the nearby Wilderness Road Regional Museum in Newbern, Virginia, Ms. Patty Manthe, a member of the Smithfield Board of Directors, and myself to visit the site on August 14, 2018.[9]

It is still a beautiful area with horses and cattle grazing. We saw where the spring flows into Thorn Spring Creek. Unfortunately, all that remains of the Floyd home itself are a few of the foundation stones.

A relative named Nicholas Jackson Floyd wrote in 1912 that within five years of the former governor's arrival, the Floyd "home and all suitable buildings were converted into an impromptu sanitarium to meet the requirements of patients from a distance, who needed and demanded protracted medical or surgical treatment."[10] Letitia was the one responsible for running the plantation and overseeing those who managed the sanitarium during the years John was away. Remembering the deaths of her three children, we conclude that she was a woman steeled in suffering and a very responsible manager.

Not surprisingly, Letitia consoled others well. Glanville was the first to publish Letitia's letter to her sister-in-law Mrs. Caroline Preston. The letter, concerning the death of Caroline's husband, William, was written from Thorn Spring on January 25, 1821. In it she writes, "He died as he lived, satisfied with the justice and goodness of his Creator. A friend to all honest men and the foe of scoundrels.... I hope God will enable his precious family to bear this sad bereavement."[11]

On January 1, 1833, Letitia wrote what Glanville calls "arguably, the singular most important historical letter." Writing to her husband, John, she reflects the frustration and even bitterness she and the governor then felt towards President Andrew Jackson. Quoting Shakespeare, she calls the president a "bloody, bawdy, treacherous, leacherous villian [sic]."[12]

Glanville and Mays thoroughly explored the reason why Floyd's friendship with Jackson turned to hatred. South Carolina challenged President Jackson with what came to be known as the Nullification Crisis. In response to what it considered an unfair tariff from Congress, South Carolina threatened to withdraw from the United States effective February 1, 1833. Jackson responded by strengthening the federal forts in Charleston harbor and sending his leading general there. He planned to send troops across Virginia to South Carolina. Governor Floyd considered this an encroachment and said no federal solider would be allowed to cross Virginia to attack a sister state. Southerners felt the president was ready to arrest Governor Floyd. This was the context of Letitia's outburst.[13]

After John died in August of 1837, Letitia moved to Burke's Garden in Tazewell County, Virginia. There she lived, at first, in a log cabin on land owned by her son George Rogers Clark Floyd, who operated a store there with his brother John Buchanan Floyd.[14]

Three very important changes happened in Letitia's life while in Burke's Garden. First was her "Dear Rush" letter. Second was her attempt to bring in Catholic settlers. The third was her baptism into the Catholic Church.

When I first discovered, for me, the key paragraph from her "Dear Rush" letter, it led me to publicize Letitia Preston Floyd. Then when Jim Glanville discovered my use of it, he too realized her importance. He and his co-author, Ryan Mays, went on to thoroughly analyze the document, which is not really a letter but a family history of 32 pages. They called it "the most significant of all the writings about the early history of the Patton, Preston, Floyd, Breckinridge, and other families in Virginia, Tennessee, and Kentucky. The letter's wealth of family information has made it a famous source for genealogists."[15]

In that key paragraph, Letitia describes the books her father had arranged to be purchased in London for the use of the tutors he hired for his children:

> A good selection of the classics, ancient history, the distinguished poets of England, "The Dictionary of Arts and Sciences" a sort of encyclopedia, with much polemics and many religious productions constituted the libraries. I would observe that the use of these books gave to each

family possessing them a station which outranked very many wealthier families.[16]

Letitia's own "station" now allowed her to petition the Bishop of Wheeling, the Archbishop of New York, and the King of England to send Catholic families to settle in Burkes Garden. During this same time, prelates such as Bishop Joseph Cretin (1799-1857) of the Diocese of St. Paul, Minnesota, and Archbishop John Ireland (1838-1918) of the Archdiocese of St. Paul, Minnesota, were famously obtaining the movement of nearly entire villages from Europe to Minnesota.[17]

Although Letitia's letters have not yet been found, Glanville carefully researched and published the six responses to her letters that had been sent by Bishop Whelan and his subordinates. Glanville concludes: "Her motives are not readily apparent." He hoped that future scholarship will reveal those motives.[18]

Why did it take Letitia so long to join the Catholic Church? She had allowed or encouraged her three daughters and three of her four sons to join, yet she herself provoked Bishop Whelan's patience when he wrote to her on May 8, 1845, "Subdue the rebellious feelings of a proud nature.... It is now, my dear friend, the 11th hour for you, as you still have it in your power to repair much of the past, to do a vast deal of good, by acknowledging before men that Savior whom you wish to acknowledge you before his Father in heaven."[19]

Is it possible that Letitia Floyd's reasons for hesitating were the same as those shared by Thomas "Stonewall" Jackson, who during the War with Mexico spent much time investigating Roman Catholicism? It was the strangeness of the Mass in Latin and other Catholic practices that made him turn to Presbyterianism.[20] Perhaps her reasons were more in line with Abraham Lincoln, who thoroughly loved Christianity, but found the fighting among its Churches too much to bear?[21] At the same time, there were a number of noticeable conversions in the United States, especially in the northern states.[22]

Whatever the reasons for her hesitations, Letitia did respond positively to Bishop Whelan's urging. An anonymous author noted that on August 12, 1854, at her home of "Cavan" estate in Burkes Garden Bishop Whelan "had the satisfaction of receiving this lady into the Catholic Church, when she received the Holy Sacraments with the lively devotion and penitence that marks the true convert." Glanville thinks her reception was "probably near the big spring on Rhudy Branch about fifty yards north of the present-day Lutheran Church."[23]

Letitia Floyd died four months later on December 12, 1854, at age 74. She was buried next to her husband in the Lewis Family Cemetery at Sweet Springs, West Virginia (then Virginia). The same anonymous author observed "the Church has not made conquest of a more elevated spirit, a warmer heart, or a more splendid intellect than hers."[24]

Glanville was interested in the influence of Virginia's "elite" women on the abolition of slavery, quoting Elizabeth Varon's 1998 book, *We Mean to be Counted: White Women and Politics in Antebellum Virginia.* Varon does not name Letitia, but does praise her husband, saying that Governor Floyd grasped "that the political battle over slavery which Turner's Rebellions sparked was a battle for the hearts and minds of white women as well as men." Glanville then "wonders if perhaps the governor's grasp of that situation has something to do with his wife."[25]

Some might object to calling Letitia a "Pioneer Catholic Feminist," since it took her so long to complete her journey into the Catholic Church. When Alexis de Toqueville was finishing his book *Democracy in America,* he asked what was "the chief cause of the extraordinary prosperity and growing power of this nation?" He answered: "the superiority of their women."[26] Since Letitia allowed her three daughters and three of her four sons to become Catholic, I conclude that she was, at least in part of her heart, "A Pioneer Catholic Feminist."

Letitia Floyd's grave would go unmarked even longer than her husband's.

CHAPTER TWO ENDNOTES

1. Glanville, *Smithfield Review (SR)* 19:77. He is pushing for a roadside marker for the Thorn Spring home of John and Letitia: "Letitia Preston Floyd: remarkable and almost unknown," Christiansburg, Virginia *News Messenger*, June 3, 2015, 4,6, available on holstonia.org.

2. historicsmithfield.org. Letitia is included in the Preston link, "family notables."

3. Ryan Mays, "The Draper's Meadows Settlement (1746-1756) Part II," *SR* 19 (2015): 1-32. See Glanville and Mays "Letitia Preston Floyd's 'My Dear Rush' Letter," *SR* 20 (2016): 86 for her meeting Mary Draper Ingles.

4. Glanville comments on her letter from Kentucky to her mother: SR 19:80-81.

5. Glanville, *SR* ibid; "Preston-Floyd Bible Records;" *DAR* 107 (August-September 1973, 7): 695.

6. Glanville, *SR* 19:82; *DAR* 107:695. He published "Virginia's first family who lived in Christiansburg," *News Messenger* (Blacksburg, Virginia), January 23, 2019, 4. He also posted a picture of the home named "Solitude" on the Lynnside website, Table of Contents.

7. Glanville, *SR* 19:78.

8. Glanville, SR 19:82.

9. Glanville, *SR* 19:87 has two photos of his March 2014 visit. See his article "Thorn Spring and Floyds deserve historical marker," *The Southwest Times*, Pulaski, Virginia, July 3, 2015, 4, available on holstonia.org.

10. Nicholas Jackson Floyd, *Biographical Genealogies of the Virginia-Kentucky Floyd Families* (Baltimore: Williams and Wilkins, 1912) 76, cited in Glanville *SR* 19:82. A young nephew read medicine with Floyd and assisted in the dispensary. Ambler, *Life*, 81, notes the medical services were "gratuitous."

11. Glanville *SR* 19:88. When I visited Smithfield in the early 1980s, researcher Mary Tabb Johnston presented me with a copy of the letter. For an earlier bereavement letter to her brother John Preston on the death of his young daughter Mary, see Glanville *SR* 19:83.

12. Glanville, *SR* 19:97, noting Hamlet, Act 2, and the two variation spellings of lecherous and villain.

13. Glanville and Mays, *SR* 19:98-99. Previously, they presented how John and Letitia viewed the Indian Removal Act, and admired Jackson: 89-92.

14. Glanville, *SR* 19:102. He visited Burke's Garden extensively. I viewed it once, in the 1980s, from the eastern rim of the Appalachian Trail. I was stunned that it looks exactly like the round crater of an extinct volcano. However, its *Wikipedia* article makes it clear that it is the bed of an ancient sea.

15. Jim Glanville and Ryan Mays, "Letitia Preston Floyd's 'My Dear Rush' Letter," *SR* 20 (2016): 79-109, quote from page 91. He and Mays had at first accepted an early 1955 harsh assessment of Letitia's historical accuracy by Preston Davie (1881-1967), but then revised it: *SR* 19, 112.

16. Letitia Preston Floyd, "Dear Rush," in Glanville and Mays, *SR* 20:91. See Harry E. Winter, "Letitia Preston Floyd: Pioneer Catholic Feminist," *SR* 19 (2015): 138. I used her quote in the publicity sent out to the media before the dedication of her cemetery marker on August 15, 1990, "Who Is Letitia Preston Floyd." I then wrote the feminist article that began to circulate. Glanville discovered it, very helpfully edited it, and then submitted it for publication in *SR*.

17. See, for example, "Leadership, Past Bishops," website of the Archdiocese of St. Paul-Minneapolis.

18. Glanville, *SR* 19:133 (124-36). He also recommends a book by Antonia Fraser, *The King and Catholics: The Fight for Rights 1829* (London: Weidenfeld & Nicolson, 2018), with its excellent reviews by Eamon Duffy in the September 28, 2018, *The Wall Street Journal*, by Patrick Geoghegan, June 9, 2018, *The Irish Times* and Jessie Childs, June 21, 2018, *The Guardian*. The reversal of anti-Catholic laws in England in 1829 described by Fraser gives a context for Floyd and Catholicism in the U.S.A.

19. Bishop Richard Whelan to Letitia Preston Floyd, May 8, 1845, Glanville *SR* 19:131.

20. For Stonewall Jacksons's search, see sonsofthesouth.net, Stonewall Jackson, index "Catholic Church," in "A New Standard of Life," 53,

Stonewall Jackson and Mexico War, relating how he had two long interviews with the "aged Archbishop of Mexico City." A Franciscan Friar may have referred him to the archbishop.

21. For Lincoln, see Mark Noll's thorough survey "The Struggle for Lincoln's Soul," *Books and Culture Magazine of Christianity Today,* booksandculture.com, posted September 1, 1995.

22. Loughery, *Dagger John,* 245-51.

23. Glanville, *SR* 19:123, quoting an anonymous article in the English Catholic *Tablet.* Very Rev. Henry Parke specifies that she was "baptized, confirmed and anointed:" *Some Notes on the Rise and Spread of the Catholic Missions in Virginia,* 1774-1850, 16. Parke's article is long out of print with copies only in the Wheeling Diocesan Archives and the libraries of Georgetown and Holy Cross Universities.

24. Glanville, *SR* 19:123.

25. Glanville, *SR* 19:95-96, quoting Elizabeth R. Varon, *We Mean to Be Counted: White Women and Politics in Antebellum Virginia* (Chapel Hill: University of North Carolina Press, 1998), 48.

26. Alexis de Toqueville, Henry Reeve, trans., *Democracy in America,* (London: Saunders & Otley, 1835); see Harry Winter, *SR* 19:138.

— CHAPTER THREE —

Letitia Floyd Lewis (1814–1886), Leader of Appalachian Catholicism and Beyond

Letitia, the eldest daughter of John and Letitia Floyd, enjoyed the education described by her mother above. In 1832, at about age 18, she joined the Catholic Church creating a sensation, according to one historian, "throughout the state" of Virginia, and by another throughout "the country."[1] On March 19,1837, Letitia became the third wife of widower William Lynn Lewis (1799-1869). They were married at the home of their relative John B. Grayson in New Orleans, Louisiana.

Letitia Floyd Lewis, daughter of Governor John Floyd Jr. and Letitia Floyd.
used with permission of Mary Katherine Williams

Letitia and William were first cousins, so a dispensation for consanguinity was obtained from the Catholic Church. Wirt H. Wills in his introduction to the "Dear Rush" letter states regarding the Preston and Floyd families: "Marriage between cousins was fairly common in early Virginia and routinely occurred in these two families." He lists Letitia Floyd Lewis as being the daughter of second cousins John Floyd and Letitia Preston Floyd, but he does not mention Letitia Floyd Lewis and her husband William Lewis, as being first cousins. He ends his list "Consanguinity became the rule in the clan. The story of the Floyds and the Prestons is a story of two families

Old Sweet Springs Resort, Sweet Springs, West Virginia

united by blood, common interest, and public service accomplishments perhaps unparalleled in American history."[2]

From the time of their marriage in 1837 until they moved to Sweet Springs in 1848, the leading prelates of the Catholic Church, including Bishop John England of Charleston, baptized Letitia's three stepchildren from William's previous marriages and their own children born at their home "Sedly," near Columbia, South Carolina. However, more research is needed on their influence in the growth of Catholicism in their South Carolina home,[3] and indeed on the home itself.

William's paternal grandfather, William Lewis (1729-1811), was the owner of the Sweet Springs Resort, which was in its heyday when William Lynn Lewis and Letitia Floyd Lewis moved to the stone house which William's grandfather had built just to the rear of the present Lynnside mansion.

William Lewis' resort, sometimes known as Old Sweet Springs, was part of a group of six resorts high in the Allegheny section of the Appalachian Mountains, to which wealthy Southerners fled in the summer to avoid the heat, humidity, and the diseases that flourished during summer time. The popular writer Marshall Fishwick describes the route: "The whole circuit could be made in less than 170 miles. But one HAD to be at the Sweet for the last week in August and the first week in September. It was like the salmon, who knew when it was time to go back up the Columbia River."[4]

Northerners who wanted to learn the views of influential Southerners came to the resort. In 2007, the county's weekly newspaper announced the discovery of ledgers showing a visit to the resort by Napoleon's American-born grand-nephew, Jerome Bonaparte Jr. (1830-1893) and his mother, along with other famous guests. Hollywood made its way to the resort in 1928 and 1929 to produce the Academy Award film *Glorious Betsy,* that tells the story of the romance of Jerome Bonaparte and Elizabeth Patterson at the resort.[5]

The 1850 Directory for the Diocese of Wheeling mentions regarding Sweet Springs that "a church is here to be erected, chiefly by individual liberality, and a clergyman is to be placed at this point, to attend Union and other neighboring places."[6] Union, the county seat of Monroe County, is about 19 miles away from Sweet Springs.

CHAPTER THREE ENDNOTES

1. Jim Glanville, "Governor John Floyd, Letitia Preston Floyd and the Catholic Church," *The Smithfield Review (SR)* 19 (2015) 123-24, quoting Catholic historian Joseph Magri (for the state) and an author known only as "JMJ" (for the country). Available on holstonia.net.

2. Wirt H. Wills, "John Floyd, Kentucky Hero, and Three Generations of Floyds and Prestons of Virginia," *SR* 2 (1998) 41-42.

3. Harry Winter, *St. John's Catholic Chapel,* 2; Lynn Spellman, "Woodville Family," lynnside.org. Charleston Diocese Archivist Brian Fahey has been unable to find any record of the Lewis' in South Carolina: email, January 31, 2019.

4. Marshall Fishwick, *Springlore in Virginia* (Bowling Green University: Popular Press, 1978) 6. For photos, see "Sweet Springs Hotel," Historic American Buildings Survey (HABS), Library of Congress, available on Sweet Springs, West Virginia Wikipedia; also Spellman and Glanville's website lynnside.org. Mary Katherine Williams published a thorough description of the resort: *Sweet Springs: Travel Guide and History* (Paint Bank, Virginia: PaintBank Press, LCC, 2009) 32-57. She is publishing a new and expanded edition of this most valuable book

5 Jett Wilson (a direct descendant of William Lewis), "Bonaparte was a Guest at Old Sweet," *The Monroe Watchman,* Union, West Virginia, August 16, 2007, 1. The ledgers are being digitalized: wilsonlewisfa-mil.com/ledgervid1h.html. In the 1980s, *The Watchman* (established 1872) still published notes of visitors coming to their family and friends in the Sweet Springs area, especially during the summer. See Mary Katherine Williams, *Sweet Springs: Travel Guide and History* 38-39 for the film.

6. My thanks to then diocesan archivist Sr. Margaret Brennan, S.S.J., who furnished me with this data.

— CHAPTER FOUR —

Letitia Lewis Builds St. John's Chapel, and the Lynnside Mansion, Sweet Springs, West Virginia

We face some difficulty in determining the actual date of completion of St. John's Chapel, but not of the Lynnside Manor. The date usually given for the chapel "to be built" is 1853, but as the Wheeling Diocesan Archivist wrote "The possibility of a temporary chapel being erected around 1853" cannot be ruled out.[1] In 1991, Michael Pauley submitted a proposal to the National Register of Historic Places to have the chapel, the manor, and the two cemeteries added to the National Register for Sweet Springs. At that point, only the resort was listed. He stated the chapel was "constructed sometime between 1853 and 1859 (most probably the earlier date)."[2]

Pauley firmly states "The manor of 'Lynnside' was constructed in 1845 on the site of the previous manor, called by the same name, that dated from c. 1800."[3]

The 1854 Diocesan Catholic Directory first mentions Fr. J. H. Walters in connection with Sweet Springs stating that he "is temporarily residing here. A brick chapel is being erected." But the first entry in the baptismal register, in Fr. Walter's hand, is for November 13, 1853. In the year 1854 there were 99 people baptized, and the numbers increase steadily until 1860, when 174 people were baptized.

Fr. Walters seems to have been at St. John the Evangelist Church in Summersville in 1858. The diocesan directory for that year lists Sweet Springs as vacant, yet the baptismal register, in Fr. Walter's handwriting, lists 124 baptisms that year. In the directory for 1859, Fr. Walters is back at Sweet Springs, visiting Union and White Sulphur Springs. The diocesan directory for the year 1860 lists Fr. Daniel O'Connor as pastor, with Lewisburg visited,

Lynnside mansion as viewed from the cemetery.
The roof of the root cellar can be seen to the left of the mansion.

yet still all the entries in the baptism and marriage registers are by Fr. Walters, right up until 1868, when Fr. Hugh McMenamin's entries appear.[4]

Who is Fr. Walters? We know from diocesan records that Walters died on August 1, 1880, in his 66th year, with no birth date given. That would make his birth year circa 1814. His obituary gives his first name as John. Diocesan records have him traveling to celebrate Mass in Charleston and "Salt Works" in Kanawha County, and even serving as pastor of St. Augustine, Grafton in 1861, when he was still residing in Sweet Springs. From Grafton he served the people of St. Peter's in Fairmont on the second and fourth Sunday of each month until the appointment of St. Peter's first pastor in 1873. Walters remained in Grafton until 1877.[5]

So from 1854 to 1868, Fr. Walters operated out of Sweet Springs. When we consider the number of baptisms and weddings that are recorded during that period, and the funerals of those buried in the two cemeteries on the knoll behind the mansion, as well as his constant travels, we can truly name Fr. Walters as the Founding Father of Catholicism in much of western Virginia and the eastern part of West Virginia.

Mrs. Spellman described the Lynnside mansion as it existed in the mid-1800s.

> The structure of the house was comprised of three floors, basement, first floor, second floor and third, or attic with small bedrooms and open space. The basement consisted of a huge kitchen and a hall pantry with a dumbwaiter. A play and gaming room, a long dance floor where the family entertained guests, and a workshop completed the basement floor. The first floor had a small back hall behind an arch from which rose a double landing staircase. The reception hall had two ornate crystal chandeliers, and was beautifully furnished. The living room extended the entire side of the house, its fourteen-foot bookcases were considered to be unusual and interesting. The dining room was furnished with sideboards and contained

> an excellent library. The second floor contained five bedrooms, all beautifully furnished.[6]

The Lynnside mansion and St. John's Chapel are about a quarter of a mile apart and visible from each other, the mansion on the southwest side of West Virginia Route 3 and the chapel on the northeast side. Together they became the center of Catholicism for about 75 years. Mrs. Spellman summed it up, most likely quoting her Aunt Coralie Lewis:

> Our little church has been honored, from time to time, by the august presence of many of the greatest dignitaries of Our Holy Mother Church—Bishop Keene of Richmond, Bishop Keane of Wheeling, our own Bishop Donaghue (this is probably James Donohue, the third Bishop of Wheeling, who died in 1922) Bishop J. O'Connell of Richmond, former rector of the Catholic University, Bishop Keily of Savanah, Archbishop Jansenns of New Orleans, and above all our venerated and well beloved Cardinal James Gibbons—names of which to be proud on the Rostrum of our little church.[7]

In 1858, Bishop McGill of Richmond made the journey to Sweet Springs to preside at the December 8 marriage of Susan Massie Lewis to Alfred J. Frederick of St. Matthew's parish in South Carolina. The following year Bishop Whelan, then in Wheeling, West Virginia, came to preside at the October 19, 1859, marriage of their second oldest daughter, Letty Preston Lewis, to her cousin Thomas Lewis Preston Cocke of Cumberland County, Georgia.

The many Irish workers who had built the Old Sweet Springs resort, the slaves who probably made and laid the bricks for the church of St. John, and the wealthy family of Letitia Floyd Lewis all worshipped together. Whether the Catholic slaves were segregated in the upstairs choir loft is unknown.

However on June 21, 1978, during the restoration of the chapel, a local contractor named Rich Mundell was presenting his work to the St. Charles Borromeo Parish Association in nearby White Sulphur Springs. His remarks received extensive coverage in the

Fr. John H. Walters
coutesey of the Diocese of Wheeling-Charleston, West Virginia

local newspapers. He said black Catholics there had told him that a leper had been given hospitality by the Lewis family in the upstairs room over the sacristy in the church. Mundell preserved the mark of the chimney exit for the stove which had heated that room, supposedly to give warmth to the leper during the wintertime.[8]

The baptismal record register for St. John's lists 99 people for 1854. The numbers increase steadily until 1860, when 174 were baptized. The 1858 register includes Letitia and William Lynn Lewis's eldest son, William Ignatius Lynn Lewis, and their eldest daughter, Susan Massie Lewis, as sponsors for their cousin Frederick Lawrence Holmes.

In addition to these two children, and William's three children by his first wife, William and Letitia had three more children of their own: Laetitia Preston, John Floyd, and Charles.[9]

When I became pastor at St. John's in 1982, the original baptismal and marriage register still existed in the sacristy. In 1983 I proposed to Lynn Spellman that we read the first names in the register during our Christmas Eve Mass on December 24th of that year, and Mrs. Spellman agreed to my proposal. We did so, after turning off the electric lights and with each participant holding a small lit candle. I read the 19 names of those baptized before Christmas Eve in 1853 beginning with the name of Margaret Sullivan—born August 23, 1853, daughter of John Sullivan and Ellen Hagerty, sponsors Dennis Callighan and Honora Callihan, baptized by Rev. J. H. Walters on November 13th. We then extinguished the candles and sang "Silent Night." The reading of the names became the policy in the church every Christmas Eve until I was transferred in July of 1991.

General David Hunter's devastation of the Lynnside mansion during the Civil War occurred in1864. The following description is by an eyewitness to the ransacking, then visiting the Lewis family at Lynnside, who wrote to her daughter on July 1, 1864:

> Then came the plundering vandals by tens and twenties, and through the whole day, destruction went on. Sometimes fifty or maybe one hundred into the house at once. They broke open every press, trunk or bureau, carried off nearly everything of any value, got everything we had to eat, not a crumb of anything being left from the basement to the garret. No—not enough to feed a bird.

St. John's Chapel, Sweet Springs, West Virginia

> Took all of her silver, except the spoons which were left out when the silver was put away and which one of the servants hid. All other jewelry, tore up and carried away every towel and napkin but six, nearly every pillow-case, sheets and blankets, destroyed nearly all of Col. Lewis' clothes, and carried off all of our underclothes.... Nearly all of our stockings are gone, all of our pocket-handkerchiefs, they even took our tooth-brushes. They destroyed the great portion of the medicines in the house, pulled our [sic] everything helter-skelter on the floors of the room, destroyed and carried out books and papers.... In fact, so much was stolen, that it is easier for me to tell you what is left.[10]

Marshall Fishwick cites a U.S. Army private as recording in his diary how Lynnside "was ransacked from top to bottom... The boys acted like madmen and destroyed much that was of no use to them. They found wine and other liquors of which they partook freely."[11]

Lynn Spellman had described her ancestor's action during the vandalizing:

> The lady of the house, being a brave and resourceful woman, repeatedly put out the fires set by the drunken soldierst (sic) until the troops left, leaving little for the residents to use for food or fuel. The livestock, having been either destroyed or driven off, Mrs. Lewis had someone follow behind and retrieve a colt when he trailed behind the other horses so they would have something to pull a plow and raise a crop.[12]

I strongly suspect that the Lewis' contact with the resort before the Civil War resulted in the few Catholics and many non-Catholics returning to their homes impressed by the faith of Letitia Floyd Lewis and her husband, William Lynn Lewis. For example, Letitia Elizabeth Garibaldi, born September 28, 1865, was baptized July 8, 1866, with William Lynn Lewis and Letitia Preston Lewis as her sponsors. The child's father was John Garibaldi (1831-1914), who was born in Genoa, and had served in the Confederate Army. Garibaldi's wife, Sarah Pori (1834-1909), received 38 letters from him during his service in the army, which included his imprisonment twice by Union forces.

Were John Garibaldi and Sarah Pori at Old Sweet as part of the summer visitors, or was he part of General David Hunter's devastation of Lynnside during the Civil War? It might even have been both.[13]

THE SPRING RESORTS AND APPALACHIA

Today the two current active resorts of the original six on the circuit, The Greenbrier in White Sulphur Springs, West Virginia, and The Homestead in Hot Springs, Virginia, give some idea of what the other resorts, especially the Sweet Springs Resort, were like up until World War II. If the vision of West Virginia and western Virginia is one of hillbillies and coal miners, then these resorts were islands of affluence and education in the middle of Appalachia.

But if we look at the two poetic pastoral letters written by the 24 bishops of Appalachia in 1975 and 1996, then even that stereotype has to be corrected.[14] Catholic historian David O'Brien has called the pastoral letter *This Land Is Home To Me* "certainly the most remarkable document of the post-conciliar American Church."[15] In 2015, the lay people of the Catholic Committee of Appalachia published their own pastoral letter.[16] Then Fr. Tom Rosica, CSB, and Sebastian Gomes produced an award-winning video about the pastoral.[17]

When Letitia Floyd Lewis's father died in the root cellar next to her mansion in August of 1837, what had prevented her from baptizing him? (Although she and her husband did not move from South Carolina to Sweet Springs until 1848, it is probable they spent summers at Lynnside). She undoubtedly knew how to baptize, and that it should be done if he was at all interested. Did the possibility of him having a contagious disease prevent her from baptizing her father due to her responsibility for her young step-children and children? Could she have asked a servant or slave to do it? Unfortunately, when General David Hunter's Union forces vandalized the mansion during the Civil War, many records were destroyed. Then in 1933, a fire inside the home eliminated the second and third floors, and thus more records were lost.[18]

CHAPTER FOUR ENDNOTES

1. Sr. Margaret Brennan, S.S.J., cited in Harry E. Winter, *A Short History of St. John's Chapel*, 1994.

2. Michael J. Pauley, National Register of Historic Places Registration Form, 1991, Section 7. See lynnside.org, external links for this valuable document of 23 pages of text, maps, and photos.

3. Pauley, National Register, Section 7, 2.

4. This data furnished by then diocesan archivist Sr. Margaret Brennan, S.S.J., and used in the various editions of *St. John's Chapel History*.

5. I am grateful to the current archivist of the diocese, Jon-Erik Gilot, who used the "Find a Grave Memorial" for Fr. Walters: email from Gilot to Winter, March 11, 2021.

6. Lynn Spellman, "Lynnside: Lewis Ancestral Home," lynnside.org. See the website for photos of the mansion as it is today from West Virginia Rt. 3, and from before the 1930s. For a longer description of the mansion, see Mary Katherine Williams, *Sweet Springs: Travel Guide and History*, (Paintbank Press, LLC, 2009), 76-77.

7. Lynn Spellman, quoted in Harry Winter, *St. John's Catholic Chapel*, 5.

8. Harry Winter, *St. John's Catholic Chapel*, 6. No slaves are listed in the 1850 census for the Lewis': Jim Glanville and Ryan Mays, "Letitia Preston Floyd: Supplementary Notes," *The Smithfield Review (SR)* 20 (2016) 73, available on holstonia.net.

9. Brock, *Virginia and Virginians*, 163.

10. Williams, *Sweet Springs: Travel Guide and History*, 78-79.

11. Marshall Fishwick citing Private William B. Start, 34th Regiment Massachusetts Volunteers, *Springlore in Virginia* (Bowling Green State U: Popular Press, 1978) 176.

12. This statement by Lynn Spellman was posted on the Lynnside website as of August 6, 2008. It is no longer available there. Accessed at lynnside.com/Lynnside.html on March 13, 2021.

13. Garibaldi's letters are available at the Virginia Military Institute website.

14. Catholic Bishops of Appalachia, *This Land Is Home To Me* (Webster Springs, West Virginia, 1975); *At Home in the Web of Life* (Webster Springs, West Virginia, 1996). For the 20th anniversary of *This Land,* see Edwin Daschbach, SVD, *Photo Essay: This Land Is Home To Me,* (Techny, Illinois: Society of the Divine Word, 1999).

15. David O'Brien, quoted by Joseph Hacala, S.J., in Daschbach, *Photo Essay,* ii.

16. The Catholic Committee of Appalachia, *The Telling Takes Us Home: Taking Our Place in the Stories That Shape Us, A People's Pastoral from the Catholic Committee of Appalachia* (Spencer, West Virginia: 2015).

17. Fr. Tom Rosica, CSB and Sebastian Gomes, *Magisterium of the People,* 2018, saltandlighttv.org.

18. When I gained entrance to the boarded up home in about 1985, I was startled to see books and pages scattered all over the floor. It is unlikely that Lynn Spellman gathered these before selling the estate to the new owner.

— CHAPTER FIVE —

Lewis Family Cemetery and Old Catholic Cemetery, Restored, Then Abandoned

It is odd that Letitia Floyd Lewis's parents' graves were left unmarked during her lifetime. She may have helped with the remarkable memorial to Dennis Stack in the Lewis Family Cemetery. Stack had died on May 20, 1847, at age 27, and his stone memorial has eight lines consoling him for dying far from his native Ireland.[1]

As one enters the Lewis Family Cemetery, a large cairn marks the grave of William Lewis (1724-1811). William was the grandfather of William Lynn Lewis.

Lynn Spellman was the owner of the mansion and the land around it, and presumably the cemetery as well. She had thought that she owned the entire cemetery of about one acre with 175 graves. However, I discovered that in 1882 the Diocese of Wheeling had purchased the back .82 acre, and had begun burying there (now about 90 of the total graves.). Spellman was as surprised by this information as the diocese was when they discovered in 1977 that Spellman, not the diocese, owned the chapel.[2]

Spellman had kept both cemeteries mowed, but those who did the mowing had damaged many of the markers. As both of us grew in awareness of the importance of the two cemeteries, we agreed to hire a professional archaeologist to investigate the site. Spellman and the Diocese hired Kenneth Robinson, a highly recommended archeologist, who spent the weeks of September 26, 1988, and June 11, 1990, probing in the two cemeteries.

Robinson's 32-page report, with 11 pages of photos, and a 5-page appendix with a map showing where each grave is, concludes with his discovery that Governor Floyd's marker was not over the site of his coffin. So the marker was moved 4 feet west and 2 feet north of its original location. Letitia's grave was definitely on the right side. In the presence of the Bishop of the Diocese of Wheeling, the Most Rev. Bernard Schmitt, many members of the Floyd Family, staff from Smithfield, and a television crew from Roanoke, Virginia, Robinson described his conclusion.

> In 1988, the area to the south and west of Governor Floyd's marker was archaeologically excavated to determine if Letitia Floyd's grave might be identified. Two grave pits were located within the excavated area. Both graves were similarly outlined with stones and their proximity, similar size, and similar condition seemed to indicate they were related, and that they were the graves of Mr. and Mrs. Floyd.[3]

The height of the restoration of these two very important cemeteries occurred on August 15, 1990, when the graves of Governor Floyd and his wife were definitively marked as shown below. The large concrete slab for the governor, which is 3 feet wide, 6 feet long, and 10 inches thick, was installed by Coralie Lewis in the 1930s. It reads:

GOV. JOHN FLOYD
TWICE GOVERNOR OF
VIRGINIA
AN APOSTLE OF SECESSION
AND THE FATHER OF
THE OREGON COUNTRY
DIED AUG. 21, 1837

Lynn Spellman and I agreed on installing a matching marker for his wife:

LETITIA PRESTON FLOYD
WIFE OF GOVERNOR JOHN FLOYD
MOTHER OF GOV. JOHN BUCHANAN FLOYD
AUTHOR AND EDUCATOR
DIED DEC. 12, 1852

Jackie Spellman, a member of the newest generation of descendants of Governor John and Letitia Preston Floyd

Bishop Schmitt blessed the new marker for Letitia and stood on exact spot where Bishop Whelan had visited the graves on October 19, 1859.[4]

Lynn Spellman's daughter Jacqueline (Jackie) was 13 years old at the time of the blessing. As the youngest present, she represented the newest generation of descendants of Governor and Letitia Preston Floyd.

Towards the end of her life, Lynn Spellman sold the mansion and much of the land. The new owner has been most cordial in allowing approach to the cemetery across his property. Apparently Spellman sold the Lewis Family Cemetery to another family in Covington, Virginia, about 25 miles from Sweet Springs. Glanville was trying to contact them prior to his death.[5]

With the current prevalence of ticks carrying Lyme disease in heavy weeds and brush, the two cemeteries are dangerous to enter after early spring and until the first hard frost in the autumn. Glanville had approached the Catholic Chaplain at Virginia Tech, near Smithfield, explaining the Preston connection. So far, no work groups of students have been able to begin the task of restoring the cemeteries.[6]

The Lewis Family Cemetery is now an orphan cemetery. With the closing of St. John's Chapel, except for an annual August 15th Mass, the Old Catholic Cemetery has sadly deteriorated too.

Coordinating the work of Robinson with volunteers from our parish and the community was one of the high points of my nine-year ministry in West Virginia. To see the two cemeteries overgrown with brush today, and much of Robinson's work invisible, is heartbreaking.

GRAVES OF BLACK AND IRISH IN THE CEMETERIES

One of the startling markers in the Lewis Family Cemetery is inscribed for the "FAITHFUL SLAVES TOM & DINAH DIED A.D.1800."[7] During our August 15 celebrations, black Catholics who formerly served the Woodville Family in Sweet Springs and now live in White Sulphur Springs, approached me to tell me that their grandparents buried an infant girl in one of the cemeteries.

In addition to the monument to Dennis Stack described at the beginning of this chapter, many of the monuments in the Lewis Family Cemetery mention the place of origin in Ireland for the deceased: two from County Mayo, three from County Kerry, two from Dingle, as well as ones from Parish Crosmaliny, Castletown County, County Cork, Ballinacourty, and Dispoil Parrish [sic].[8]

IRISH CLERGY AND THE RELIGIOUS FROM SWEET SPRINGS

The Stack Family has furnished priests and nuns from every generation since the mid 1800s. Thomas Stack, nephew of Dennis, born in the Sweet Springs area on July 3, 1845, was ordained in the Jesuits in 1881. He became a very popular professor at Boston College, and was chosen president of the college in the summer of 1887. He died on August 30, 1887.[9] His sisters Elizabeth and Margaret became nuns in the community of St. Vincent de Paul. A plaque at the entrance to St. John's Chapel memorializes all three.

The last member of this family to become a priest was Robert Howe, who was ordained for the Diocese of Richmond, Virginia. He died on June 12, 2015.[10]

Fr. Paul Hickey of the Diocese of Wheeling, and cousin Mary Claire, CSJ, of the Sisters of St. Joseph, Wheeling, are descended from Sweet Springs Irish Catholics. Hickey was ordained on May 26, 1956. He died November 8, 1998.[11] Sr. Mary Claire made her profession on August 17, 1955. She died on January 20, 2016.[12]

We have no direct record that Letitia Floyd Lewis contributed to the education and formation of the priests and nuns who

Grave marker for
"Faithful Slaves Tom & Dinah"
photo by Jim Glanville

came from Sweet Springs, but it would be highly unusual if the Lewis family did not, in the customary ways, encourage their vocation.

Rosalind Lewis, described by Mary Katherine Williams as the "biographer of the Lewis family," records that Letitia "even in her old age, in those primitive times, she served as doctor whenever needed and regardless of the distance or of the time of day or night, she would saddle her horse and go out."[13]

Fr. Walters was sent to Sweet Springs in 1853 as his first assignment, having been ordained by Bishop Whelan on August16 of that year, when he was about 39 years old.[14] Letitia Floyd Lewis was definitely 39 years old at that time, and her husband, William Lynn Lewis, was 54. Hopefully we may some day find letters from one of them showing the relationship between the three. Remember that Letitia's brothers and sisters visited Lynnside often, especially during the last week of August and the first week of September. With Fr. Walters residing in the mansion, we may presume they all saw a great deal of each other, even though Fr. Walters traveled extensively.

If Fr. J. H. Walters is rightly called the Founder of Catholicism in this part of what is now West Virginia, which includes much of western Virginia, then it is certain that Letitia Floyd Lewis should be rightly called the Foundress.[15]

Letitia's father and her father's cousin, Charles Floyd's influence had extended to the Oregon Territory and back through Iowa to Virginia. Now Letitia's and her siblings' influence traveled south to Georgia, South Carolina, southern Virginia, and on to West Virginia, Kentucky, and Tennessee.

LEWIS FAMILY AND OLD CATHOLIC CEMETERIES LINK WITH METHODIST OLD REHOBOTH CHURCH/MUSEUM AND CONFERENCE CENTER

About 16 miles away, on Route 3 West towards Union, stands the Old Rehoboth Church, built in 1786, and its cemetery. The log cabin-style Methodist church is an important historic site known for being the oldest existing church building in West Virginia. The Rehoboth Church and Museum, built in 1976, contain two unusual metal plates. One of them describes a surveying instrument, and the other is inscribed as follows:

EUGENE P. KEENAN.
SON OF EUGENE BURKE KEENAN.
SON OF A.M. (MAC) KEENAN.
SON OF PHLLIP DUFFY KEENAN.
SON OF ANDREW KEENAN.
SON OF ROBERT KEENAN.
SON OF EDWARAD KEENAN.
SON OF PATRICK KEENAN.

THE STORY IS. WHEN PATRICK EMIGRATED
FROM IRELAND, BOARDING THE BOAT A
CATHOLIC PRIEST. HE LEFT THE BOAT.
MARRIED TO MY GREAT.GREAT.GREAT.
GREAT.GREAT.GREAT. GRANDMOTHER.[16]

During my pastorate at Union, the Methodists always asked to borrow a pair of rosary beads for their annual play. The play was set in 1786, and in it Edward Keenan's Catholic mother-in-law, Griselda Donally, conspicuously prayed her rosary during the visits of the Methodist preacher.[17]

Did Letitia Floyd have any contact with the immigrant Irish or the Methodists in the Union area? No documentation has yet been found, but it would be odd if she did not.

Old Rehoboth Church, Union, West Virginia

Griselda Donally was buried outside the regular cemetery grounds at Old Rehoboth, probably at her own request. Several, probably non-Catholic relatives, were buried outside the Old Catholic Cemetery grounds as well.[18]

Glanville sent the Keenan matter to historian Gerald Fogarty S.J., who replied that he knew of only one other Irish Catholic priest during this ante-bellum period who joined a Protestant Church.[19] If we look at the French and Bohemian priests (St. John Neumann came to the United States because there were too many priests in Bohemia), who came during those years, the number may be much higher. It is possible Catholics have limited the search to our own diocesan archives. Would we be surprised if we asked the archivists of Protestant frontier Churches to research this too?

CHAPTER FIVE ENDNOTES

1. Stack text in Kenneth Robinson, *Archaeological Investigation of the Letitia Preston Floyd and Gov. John Floyd Graves and Documentation of the Lewis Family-Old Catholic Cemetery Sweet Springs, Monroe County, West Virginia* (February 15, 1991); lynnside.org.

2. The Diocese paid Spellman $1.00 for the chapel's ownership to be legally transferred.

3. Kenneth Robinson, *Archaeological Investigation,* 9-10, lynnside.org. For a description of the Lewis Family Cemetery before the restoration started, see Harry E. Winter, "Progress and Preservation at Sweet Springs," *Preservation Alliance Newsletter* (West Virginia), Spring, 1985, 3-4.

4. Harry Winter, O.M.I., "Letitia Preston Floyd: Pioneer Catholic Feminist," *The Smithfield Review (SR)* 19 (2015), 143, edited by Jim Glanville, available on holstonia.net; original version on lynnside.org.

5. Glanville, map of properties formerly owned by Lynn Spellman, showing the Lewis Family Cemetery to be owned by James and Jeremy Skidmore, Cemetery Folder.

6. Glanville met with the Newman Club Chaplain, Fr. David Sharland, October 17, 2014. Working with the Greenbrier Valley Council Knights of Columbus was discussed; Cemetery Folder.

7. Photo by Jim Glanville, August 15, 2016; description in Robinson, *Archaeological Investigations,* 20, 25; Harry Winter, *St. John's Catholic Chapel,* 9; photo to be on Lynnside website, currently Winter, "Return to Appalachia, 2016," omiusa.org.

8. Robinson, *Archaeological Investigations,* Lewis Family Cemetery, Part II, 4-5; Cemetery Folder.

9. Charles F. Donovan, *History of Boston College* (Chestnut Hill, Massachusetts: University Press of Boston College, 1990) p. 89; archive.org/details/historyofbostonc00dono_0.

10. Obituary, Robert "Bob" Howe, Seaver Funeral Home, June 12, 2015.

11. Harry Winter, personal communication from Fr. Hickey, during the publicity for the rededication of St. John's Chapel, 1982; *St. John's Catholic Chapel*, 9. Wheeling Diocesan Archivist Jon-Erik Gilot to Harry Winter, January 29, 2019.

12. Sr. Mary Palmer, CSJ to Harry Winter, email February 13, 2019.

13. Mary Katherine Williams, *Sweet Springs: Travel Guide and History*, 20, 85, quoting Rosalind Williamson Lewis, Lewis (Private, 1969), 125. Collections at Virginia State Library.

14. Wheeling Diocesan Archivist Jon-Erik Gilot, email to Harry Winter, March 11, 2021.

15. Winter, *St. John's Catholic Chapel*, 3.

16. Copy of plate furnished to me by then curator Ken Stockwell, during my visit of August 15, 2009. The second plate, slightly smaller, describes the attached surveying instrument of A.M. (Mac) Keenan. Old Rehoboth has a *Wikipedia* page, but its own with the West Virginia Methodist Church is under revision. See travelmonroe.com/old rehoboth.pdf for a short, attractive description.

17. Joyce Ancrile, *Rehoboth, A Play in Two Acts*, Commission on Archives and History, West Virginia Conference of the United Methodist Church, 1976. Anita Tracy, the curator who sent me this, said "Some parts need to be revised." There is also some confusion as to whether Patrick or Edward is the priest.

18. Anita Tracy to Harry Winter, August 14, 2016; The West Virginia Cemetery Preservation Alliance lists those buried in the regular cemetery: wvcpaweb.org/cemeteryregister/Monroe/MonroeOldRehob.html. See Robinson, *Archaeological Investigations*, map, for the Old Catholic Cemetery.

19. Jim Glanville to Gerald Fogarty, email; Fogarty to Glanville; Glanville to Harry Winter, all July 29, 2016.

— CHAPTER SIX —

Benjamin Rush Floyd (1811-1860), Freedom of Conscience Before John F. Kennedy

John Floyd Jr.'s son Benjamin Rush Floyd not only attended the prep school for Georgetown University when his congressman father took him and his older brother to Washington, D.C., he also attended Georgetown University. His brother-in-law United States Senator John Johnston describes that Benjamin "graduated with great distinction and where he is still remembered and spoken of as the best pupil ever at the college."[1] Benjamin's mother wrote a letter to the editor of a Baltimore based, weekly news magazine, enclosing her letter to Dr. Benjamin Rush concerning her son Benjamin, who had been named after the doctor. She informed the editor that due to Rush's skill as a doctor, her "little family owes the lives and health of both parents."[2] She also enclosed Dr. Rush's reply that includes this advice to his namesake:

> May you be kept by a kind Providence from all the errors and follies that characterized my youth.... begin in childhood, to honor and obey your parents, to learn your catechism, and to commit passages in the Bible to memory. As you advance in life, go constantly to a place of worship.[3]

Bailey asserts that Benjamin Rush Floyd "made his submission at Saint Peter's in Richmond while he was serving in the Legislature in 1851."[4] He would have been about 40 years old at that time.

In 1852 while Benjamin Rush Floyd was running for election as a circuit court judge, he responded to an anti-Catholic slur from J. Pepper with a defense of his faith that might have impressed John F. Kennedy. That was during a time when one of the Know Nothing Movement's tenets was the danger of Catholicism, as his contemporaries noticed.[5]

Glanville reproduces Pepper's 17-line letter of February 14, 1852. His key accusation was that as rumored Catholic, Floyd could do what he pleased, and the priest would forgive him of his sins for a few dollars. Floyd responded on February 20, 1852, with a letter totaling almost five full pages. The key text is below:

> The great American principle—the Jeffersonian rule—that which more than all other things distinguishes our form of government from all others, is the principle of religious freedom.... In becoming a member of the Catholic Church I have but done that which every other citizen who professes to be member of any other Christian denomination has done, or ought to have done—exercised my own reason and pursued the dictates of my own conscience. For that I am answerable to God alone.[6]

He spent about a page and a half addressing the issue of payment of money to forgive sins, calling it "a piece of ridiculous nonsense." He went on to view it as "only one of a hundred similar stories, equally groundless, equally ridiculous, which are daily circulated of the Catholic religion. Nothing seems too absurd to find some one to credit it." He reminded Pepper "that multitudes of the wisest, best and greatest men of the world have been members of the Catholic church," citing Lafayette, "at the head of a Catholic army stood side by side with Washington and his patriot troops and drove the Protestant army of England from the soil of Virginia." He concluded "a more upright, just, or learned jurist never graced the American bench than the present amiable and pious Catholic chief justice of the United States."[7] The pious Catholic chief justice he was referring to was Roger B. Taney.

Floyd was defeated in the election for circuit judge, but in 1857 he was elected to the legislature of Virginia representing Wythe county. Johnston believes "the single session he served was one of the most important that ever assembled in Virginia." Legislation which Floyd championed paid for railroads to be built that united the central and western portions of the state.[8]

Benjamin spent much time in Burkes Garden, which was one reason his mother moved there. He and his wife, Nancy, took over a home in Wytheville that was built in 1852, and was named "Oak Level" by its first occupants. His wife changed the name of the house to "Loretto," after the sanctuary in Italy. A local historian wrote, "His name shall ever be handed down from generation to generation in connection with his efforts to establish a Catholic mission in Wytheville."[9]

Bishop Whelan consecrated the Catholic mission as St. Mary's Church in 1845. It was known at the "Cathedral in the Wilderness," being the main Catholic Church between Lynchburg, Virginia and Bristol, Tennessee. Another historian elevates Floyd to "prominence on the state level," and after listing his many civic accomplishments, includes part of an obituary written for Floyd: "He was a lawyer, as a scholar, or as an eloquent and gifted political speaker he had but few equals in the State. For the spotless purity of his private and public life he stood without rival anywhere."[10]

Bailey records that Floyd occupied the same pew in St. Peter's Church, Richmond that Supreme Court Chief Justice Roger Taney did when Taney visited Richmond.[11]

The 2019 discussion in Virginia of Governor Henry Wise's role in the destruction of the Know Nothing Party when he campaigned against it in 1855 reminds us that the Catholic Floyd may have been influential in Wise's campaign. More research is needed.[12]

Floyd's brother-in-law Senator John Johnston also describes Benjamin Rush Floyd's death. Floyd was visiting the home of his brother John B. Floyd in Washington County, Virginia, when he had "a spasm of the heart and died before either a priest or doctor could reach him."[13]

CHAPTER SIX ENDNOTES

1. Senator John Johnston, "Benjamin Rush Floyd, The Sons of Gov. John Floyd," *The John P. Branch Historical Papers of Randolph-Macon College*, ed. Charles H. Ambler, (Richmond, Virginia: Richmond Press, 1913) 4:105. Online at books.google.com/books?id=MBsLAAAAIkAAJ.

2. Jim Glanville and Ryan Mays, "A Sketch of Letitia Preston Floyd and Some of Her Letters," *The Smithfield Review (SR)* 19 (2015) 85, for the text of her letter to the editor. Her original letter is not quoted.

3. Dr. Benjamin Rush Floyd to Master Benjamin Rush Floyd, April 21, 1812 (he was a little over four months old). Glanville reproduces the entire letter: SR 19:85-86, and comments on its importance to baseball historians in his article "The Founding Father and the Christiansburg Baby," *News Messenger* (Christiansburg, Virginia), 4, February 26, 2014, on lynnside.org.

4. James H. Bailey, *A History of the Diocese of Richmond, The Formative Years* (Richmond: Chancery Office, 1956) 66.

5. Johnston, *The John P. Branch Historical Papers* 4:78.

6. Johnston, *The John P. Branch Historical Papers* 4:109, 111; Glanville, "Benjamin Rush Floyd's Defense of His Catholic Faith," lynnside.org.

7. Johnston, *The John P. Branch Historical Papers* 4:112-13; Glanville, ibid.

8. Johnston, *The John P. Branch Historical Papers* 4:106.

9. Linda McHone Spiker, "St. Mary's Catholic Church," *Wythe County Historical Review* 50 (July 1996), 5.

10. Frederick Bittle Kegley, *Kegley's Virginia Frontier* (Roanoke, Virginia: Roanoke Historical Society, 1938), 231, 260. My gratitude to Tess Evans, History Specialist Wytheville Historical Society, for bringing Spiker and Kegley to my attention. Kegley sketches the relationship between Charles Pepper and the beverage Dr. Pepper, 261.

11. Bailey, *A History*, 66-67.

12. Editorial, "Should Henry Wise be honored?" *The Roanoke Times*, February 15, 2019. Glanville believes the editorial is based on the work of John David Bladek (without mentioning him): "Virginia Is Middle Ground: The Know Nothing Party and the Virginia Gubernatorial Election of 1855," *The Virginia Magazine of History and Biography*, 106 (Winter, 1998, 1): 35-70.

13. Johnston, *The John P. Branch Historical Papers*, 4:115.

— CHAPTER SEVEN —

The Other Floyd Children

John Floyd Jr. and Letitia Floyd had twelve children together: Susanna Smith Floyd, John Buchanan Floyd, George Rogers Clark Floyd, William Preston Floyd, George Rogers Clarke Floyd, Benjamin Rush Floyd, Letitia Preston Floyd, Eliza Lavalette Floyd, Nicketti Buchanan Floyd, Coraly Patton Floyd, Thomas Lewis Preston Floyd, and Mary Lewis Mourning Floyd.

Susanna, the first George, Coraly, Thomas, and Mary all died young. Of those who lived to adulthood, we have discussed Benjamin and Letitia. Below is information on the other Floyd children:

WILLIAM PRESTON FLOYD (1809–1870)

William Floyd's valedictory from Georgetown University upon receiving his A.B. in 1830 was "long remembered for its eloquence."[1] There is not much material available on William compared to his younger brother Benjamin Rush. It is probable he did not directly influence ante-bellum Catholicism, since United States Senator John Johnston notes William became a Catholic "in the latter part of his life."[2]

William was married first to Martha Jane Mills, and second to Frances Gilman.[3]

GEORGE ROGERS CLARKE FLOYD (1810–1895)

He was the second so named son, after the first died in infancy. George did not accompany his older brother William nor his younger brother Benjamin to Washington D.C. when their father served in congress. The governor in his diary for November 4, 1831, records that his wife, "and her children, William, Lavalette,

Nicketti, Corlie and Woushippakiga" arrived. Woushippakiga would seem to be a nickname for George Rogers Clarke Floyd, perhaps another indication of some Native American ancestry.[4]

George and his brother John Buchanan Floyd seem to have been the first of the family to move to Burke's Garden, where Glanville notes they were operating a store.[5] At one point they owned upwards of 3,040 acres. They sold 800 acres to their mother on June 10, 1841, and it was on that land that she built her home.[6] After serving as Secretary of the Wisconsin Territory, George moved to Logan County, West Virginia. He was elected to the state legislature at age 60. Johnston states that although Floyd had never made a speech before, his first speech in the house "electrified the body and probably astonished himself… he is now among the best public speakers in the country. Whenever he is advertised to speak, great crowds assemble to hear him… He is a Catholic."[7]

ELIZA LAVALETTE FLOYD HOLMES (1816–1887)

Eliza Lavalette Floyd probably joined her older sister Letitia in becoming a Catholic in 1832. From that point, their paths differed and then converged. In 1845, she married George Frederick Holmes, who was born in 1820 in Georgetown, British Guyana. He attended the University of Durham in England, but left for Quebec in 1837 without taking a degree.[8] Bishop Whelan shared Letitia Preston Floyd's surprise at Lavalette's choice: "With you I regret that the latter did not select a Virginian for her partner."[9]

Lavalette is mentioned at least once in five of the six letters Bishop Whelan and other Catholic leaders wrote to Lavalette's mother. She probably had a strong influence on her mother's eventual conversion.[10]

George Frederick Holmes was the first president of the University of Mississippi. He spent most of his final years teaching at the University of Virginia, where he specialized in promoting Southern culture, especially states rights and slavery. He and

Lavalette had seven children, five of whom survived into adulthood. Holmes' correspondence and diaries at Duke University may contain information about his wife.[11]

Eliza Lavalette Holmes died on September 12, 1887, and George shortly after on November 4, 1887. They both are buried in marked graves in the Lewis Family Cemetery.[12]

Further research is needed on whether George or their children were ever baptized.

NICKETTI FLOYD JOHNSTON (1819–1908)

Nicketti was the youngest of the Floyd daughters to convert to Catholicism. Her name is an historical puzzle, variously spelled Neickettie and Nickette. In a website discovered by Glanville, the author states "'Nicketti' is not an identifiable Indian name, and is probably a corruption of some other name. It could be derived from 'Necotowance,' the former name of a creek in King William [Virginia] County"[13]

After thoroughly investigating all the sources available to him in 2015, Glanville wrote to one of Governor Floyd's direct descendants and to me stating: "The word Nicketti is missing from the early MDR [My Dear Rush letter] copies made by Cochran and Holmes in the 1840s. My working conclusion is that here we have a case of 'genealogical larceny.' Some person unknown, at a time unknown, deliberately falsified the transcript to alter the historical record."[14] Glanville remained skeptical of Governor Floyd's Native American ancestry and that of his daughter Nicketti.

With DNA testing now accurate, perhaps one or more of Governor Floyd's descendants could be tested for Native American ancestry. Then the tests from both the governor and his daughter could be compared, settling the question of the Floyd family ancestry once and for all.

Nicketti's marriage to lawyer and politician John W. Johnston resulted in his becoming "a convert to the oldest Christian religion."[15]

She too is mentioned in the correspondence between her mother and Bishop Whelan, although not as frequently as Lavalette.[16]

The Johnstons had twelve children. One of them, Dr. George Ben Johnston, became a prominent physician in Richmond, Virginia.[17] Bailey notes that he "was taught the precepts and imbued with the devoutness of the Roman Catholic Church."[18]

In 1867, Nicketti founded, with her husband's help, Villa Maria Academy of the Visitation, in Abingdon, Virginia, for the education of girls. In 1902, the academy was moved to Wytheville, Virginia, and renamed Visitation Academy. It closed in 1944 due to a lack of teaching nuns.[19]

Her husband's unpublished writings show great interest in the Catholic Church. When Ambler edited them in 1913, they undoubtedly caused those who read them to appreciate Catholicism more.[20] His position as a two-term United States Senator from Virginia from 1870 to 1883, the first term shortly after the Civil War, increased the influence of his wife and children.

JOHN BUCHANAN FLOYD (1806–1863)

The oldest surviving son, John Buchanan Floyd, served as the governor of Virginia from 1849 to 1852. There are a number of discrepancies concerning details of John's life. The first is the question of his attending the same Georgetown Catholic school in Washington, D.C. as his two younger brothers. *Wikipedia* lists "Georgetown University" as his first school and the "University of South Carolina, Columbia (BA)" as his second.[21] Yet nowhere in the long description of John by his brother-in-law Senator John Johnston is there any reference to a Georgetown school. Instead Johnston writes: "John Buchanan Floyd obtained his collegiate education at the South Carolina College in Columbia, his father preferring that institution to any other place."[22]

A second discrepancy concerns his entry in the *New Catholic Encyclopedia*. John was the only child of the Floyd's not to convert to Catholicism, yet strangely he is the only Floyd listed in that book. The 23-line entry does not claim him to be Catholic. Instead it describes his problems as Secretary of War under President James Buchanan, and as a confederate general under Jefferson Davis.[23]

A third discrepancy concerns any children he and his wife Sarah Preston might have had. *Wikipedia* alternates between none and a possible child. A genealogy source[24] confidently lists the birth date of a daughter, Eliza as 1825, and states "???" for the birth date of their son John Buchanan Floyd Jr. The same source affirms John Buchanan Floyd "delivered the oration at the cornerstone laying of the Washington Monument."

Clearly more research is needed on John Buchanan Floyd.

The fact that John was a Confederate general was the reason for the vandalism of his sister's mansion in Sweet Springs by Union troops. Johnston states that all the Floyd brothers and sisters were "frequent guests at Lynnside."[25] So most likely John Buchanan Floyd visited St. John's Chapel, and saw the impact of Catholicism on his siblings. I strongly suspect he is part of the Cloud of Witnesses that the Floyd and Lewis families represent.

After spending 25 pages on John Buchanan Floyd, Johnston concludes:

> Gen. Floyd had great gifts, physical and mental. His appearance always commanded attention and whenever he stopped in the street to talk, a crowd soon collected around him. He was an eloquent speaker, and very witty, interesting and instructive in conversation. He was beloved by his family and friends, but like most men of strong character had also bitter enemies. As a Southern man, in the cabinet of a Northern president, when hostilities were about to ensue, he was placed in a position where he could not escape calumny. But when the facts are known it is seen that he acted on that occasion, as on all others, with honor and wisdom.[26]

CHAPTER SEVEN ENDNOTES

1. John G. Shea, *Memorial of the First Centenary of Georgetown University* (Washington, D.C.: Published for the College by P.F. Collier, 1891), *seriatim,* cited by Jim Glanville, "Governor John Floyd, Letitia Preston Floyd and the Catholic Church," *The Smithfield Review (SR)* 19 (2015) , 124, available on holstonia.net.

2. Johnston, *The John P. Branch Historical Papers,* 4:103.

3. geni.com / people / William-Preston-Floyd.

4. Ambler, *Life of John Floyd,* 168; Glanville, *SR* 19:95; comment by Alex Luken, werelate.org / wiki / Person:Letitia_Preston_(2), accessed February 6, 2018. Often "Clarke" drops the "e" to Clark.

5. Glanville, *SR* 19:102.

6. Glanville, *SR* 20:71-72.

7. Johnston, *The John P. Branch Historical Papers,* 4:105.

8. "George Frederick Holmes," *Wikipedia.*

9. Bishop Vincent Whelan to Letitia Preston Floyd, Letter 5, May 8, 1845, Glanville, *SR* 19:130.

10. Glanville, *SR* 19:124-36.

11. "George Frederick Holmes: Southern Intellectual," Virginia Center for Civil War Studies, civilwar.vt.edu / wordpress / george-frederick-holmes-southern-intellectual, accessed February 5, 2019; "George Frederick Holmes Papers, 1767-1960," repository.duke.edu / dc / holmesgeorge, accessed February 5, 2019.

12. Robinson, *Archaeological Investigation,* Appendix, 3. Two Holmes are buried beside them (their children?): Henry Hendon Holmes (1853-1893) and Mennie Holmes (January 27, 1855-November 17, 1923).

13. *Pocahontas-Rolfe Celebration,* University of Virginia Special Collection, quoted on jeaniesgeneology.com / 2011 / 11 / im-related-to-princess.html, p. 9 of 16, accessed February 13, 2021.

14. Jim Glanville, emails to G. Jason Floyd and Harry Winter, between March 27, 2015, and August 9, 2015, quote from the latter. See also his "Historians and Genealogists Don't Always See Eye to Eye," Christiansburg, Virginia *News Messenger*, September 9, 2015, 4.

15. Bailey, *A History*, 66.

16. Glanville, *SR* 19:126-28.

17. John W. Johnston, *Wikipedia*.

18. Bailey, *A History*, citing "George Ben Johnston, M.D.LL.D.: An Appreciation," *Bulletin of the Medical College of Virginia* (December 1916), 3-4.

19. Historical Society of Washington County, Virginia: hswcv.org/history; pinterest.com/pin/474144667005364670.

20. Senator John Johnston, "Benjamin Rush Floyd, The Sons of Gov. John Floyd," *The John P. Branch Historical Papers of Randolph-Macon College*, ed. Charles H. Ambler, (Richmond, Virginia: Richmond Press, 1913) 4:78-115. Online at books.google.com/books?id=MBsLAAAAIkAAJ.

21. John B. Floyd, *Wikipedia*, accessed February 22, 2021.

22. Johnston, "The Sons of Governor John Floyd—John Buchanan Floyd," *The John P. Branch Historical Papers*, 4:78.

23. John Quentin Feller, Jr. (assistant archivist Archdiocese of Baltimore, Maryland), "Floyd, John Buchanan," *New Catholic Encyclopedia* (Washington, D.C., The Catholic University of America, 1967) 5:982.

24. geni.com/people/Brig-Gen-John-B-Floyd-CSA-U-S-Secretary-of-War/6000000010733126038, accessed February 22, 2021.

25. Johnston, *John P. Branch Historical Papers*, cited most recently, 1991, in Michael Pauley, National Register of Historic Places, Part 8, lynnside.org, list of external links.

26. Johnston, 4:103.

— CHAPTER EIGHT—

Conclusion: Demise or Restoration in American Catholicism and American Culture

Fr. Daniel Lord, SJ, (1888-1955) was drawn to Sweet Springs from the summer of 1932 through 1935.[1] Fr. Lord was known as the "Hollywood Priest" for his work in drafting the 1930 Production Code for motion pictures. Lord viewed his work as "a chance to read morality and decency into mass recreation." During his days in the Jesuit novitiate in St. Louis, Missouri, Lord became close friends with United State Navy Admiral Patrick M.L. Belanger, who had purchased the estate "Earlhurst," near St. John's Chapel.

Their daughter Miriam Belanger deOlloqui relates that Fr. Lord offered daily Mass in St. John's Chapel. He also directed pageants with the Belanger children, of which they have home movies. They and I offered these home movies to the Jesuits in St. Louis, in hopes of receiving some of Fr. Lord's writings that would describe his visits to Earlhurst.[2] Nothing resulted.

When Bishop Bernard Schmitt celebrated the August 15 Mass in 1990, he blessed a plaque commemorating Fr. Lord's visits to St. John's Chapel. That plaque, along with another for the Stack Priests and Nuns, and Cardinal Gibbons' visit, now hang just inside the church door.

The wedding of Miriam Belanger to Valentine deVentades deOlloqui at St. John's Chapel on October 18, 1958, was the last wedding held there before the chapel fell into disuse. After the chapel was rededicated in 1983, her daughter Miriam deOlloqui's wedding to Jack James Turner was held there on October 9, 1999. That was the last one before the chapel was closed in the early 2000s.[3]

Most Rev. Francis Bible Schulte (later archbishop of New Orleans) succeeded Bishop Hodges in 1985, and continued interest in the chapel. He solemnly took possession of it on October 4, 1986. Bishop Schulte's Act of Thanksgiving included, "I join myself to Cardinal Gibbons and all the archbishops and bishops who have visited here. Trusting in God's help, we join in a mutual act of thanksgiving to God for what He has accomplished in the house of worship during the past century and a half."

The parishioners promised to "faithfully maintain St. John's Chapel, so that our Catholic faith may be witnessed in this Sweet Springs Valley." They then recalled "the Irish immigrants, the black servants, and the landed families who together passed the faith on to us, mindful of this Cloud of Witnesses, we pledge to hold ever more dearly, and to proclaim more clearly 'One Lord, One Faith, and One Baptism.'" The words—One Lord, One Faith, and One Baptism—are inscribed over the outside door of St. John's Chapel.[4]

On April 30, 1988, Bishop Schulte confirmed five young people at St. John's Chapel. The program noted that the first bishop of Wheeling, Richard Vincent Whelan, had confirmed 20 people in St. John's on July 26, 1868, including Garribaldi [sic], Hickey, and Stack.[5]

In late 1986, I was asked to supervise the internship of the first Vietnamese priest for the diocese, That-Son Nguyen-Ngoc, who arrived on January 3, 1987. After his internship he asked, to my surprise, to be ordained to the transitional deaconate in St. John's Chapel. So on November 18, 1989, Bishop Bernard Schmitt, who had succeeded Bishop Schulte in early 1989, came to Sweet Springs for the first deaconate ordination ever in the historic chapel. The chapel was full of parishioners and the Vietnamese relatives of That-Son.[6] I could not but wonder if the Cloud of Witnesses that day might have included Letitia Floyd Lewis and her descendants.

Fr. That-Son was recently interviewed in the Jesuit edited journal *America*. The article, "Waiting for Morning in Moundsville," sums up the frustration of people of Appalachia over the way religious orders like the Oblates of Mary, the Diocese of Wheeling, and the entire nation treat them.[7] A synopsis of Oblate ministry in Appalachia, and the way lay Catholics are adapting, is ongoing.[8]

Lynn Spellman reading at the deaconate ordination of That-Son.

Bishop Schmitt attempted to find a priest replacement for the Oblates when our community leadership decided to leave Appalachia in the late 1980s. While he could not find a priest, he did find a West Virginian nun, Sister Molly Bauer, CSJ. She was installed by Bishop Schmitt as Parochial Coordinator on October 8, 1992. She resided at Union and coordinated Masses at three chapels: at St. Peter's in Peterstown, on the southern border of the county with Virginia, at the chapel of St. Andrew in Union, and at St. John's. Sister Molly was promoted to Pastoral Associate in 2001.

Sister Molly noted that she coordinated the "last regularly scheduled Mass at St. John's Chapel" on Sunday, May 29, 1994, at 3:30 pm, Bishop Schmitt presiding. Sister Molly further wrote:

> Since this faith community dates back to 1859, and since St. John's is the oldest standing catholic church [sic] in the diocese, the church building is to be preserved and occasional liturgical celebrations may be celebrated there. The church building and the two cemeteries are being assigned to St. Charles Borromeo, White Sulphur Springs.[9]

St. Peter's was sold first, and then in 2004 when Sister Molly moved to a health ministry assignment, St. Andrew's was sold.

Bishop Michael Bransfield, who had succeeded Bishop Schmitt in 2004, forbade his priests to celebrate Mass in Monroe County (except for August 15), for fear they would be overworked. So for the first time since the Oblates came in 1977, there was no official Catholic presence in the county. Of the almost 100 Catholic families present at the peak, about one third of them have joined Protestant Churches, one third go to no church, and the remaining third drive almost an hour one way over dangerous roads to attend a Catholic Church outside the county.

The Greenbrier Valley Council of the Knights of Columbus help lead the few families who struggle on to maintain a Catholic presence, especially in the county seat of Union. With Bransfield's resignation/removal in 2018, Catholics hope that our leadership's bias for cities, as opposed to small towns and rural areas, will be overcome by a new bishop.

The sale of the Sweet Springs Resort to the State of West Virginia in 1947 resulted in it becoming a personal care home, named after Andrew J. Rowan, the soldier who was raised in nearby Gap Mills, and had carried the "Message to Garcia," in the Spanish American War. There were up to five elderly Catholic women among the hundred residents of the home. The pastor from St. Charles Borromeo Church, White Sulphur Springs, was responsible for visiting the home, until March 13, 1978, when Fr. James MacGee, O.M.I. was assigned as chaplain. With the rededication of St. John's by Bishop Hodges on April 17, 1983, Mass was offered on first Fridays in the former ballroom, now the auditorium. The Catholics were driven to the weekly Saturday evening 6 o'clock Mass at St. John's, less than five minutes away.

A financial crisis caused the state to close the home and attempt to sell the buildings on December 2, 1995. Ultimately the Bank of White Sulphur Springs bought the old resort. The first person who attempted to renovate it, failed.[10]

In 1988, to end the Marian Year, the holyday Mass of August 15th was followed by an ice cream social on the lawn in front of the chapel. Photos of this Mass, which became traditional, show the women serving the ice cream dressed in bonnets and aprons in the style of the late 1880s.[11] Mike Williams of the Knights of Columbus wrote in the "Tidbits in the History" addition to the booklet about the chapel distributed at each August 15th Mass: "Traditionally the Feast of the Assumption Mass at St. John's was followed by an ice cream social."[12] I was told by many people in the Union and Sweet Springs area that after World War I on Sunday afternoons families from all the area towns would drive a circuit through Ronceverte and Lewisburg, in Greenbriar County, West Virginia, to Union and Sweet Springs in Monroe County, and through White Sulphur Springs in Greenbriar County. Along the way, they would stop for ice cream at the many small stores. So Sweet Springs was well-known.

R.R. Reno, editor of *First Things* noted an event following the Mass on August 15, 2015: "'The remains of John Anthony Diehl were laid to rest at the St. John's Catholic Church cemetery in Sweet Springs, West Virginia Saturday, August 15. John died in his mother's womb at five months. He is survived by his parents, William and Mary, and seven siblings, Kevin, Jarod, Alaina, Sydney, Emily, Joseph, and Vincent, all of Durham, North Carolina.' May John Anthony rest in peace."[13]

Monsignor John Williams, Vicar for Priests in the Diocese of Raleigh, North Carolina, who has a seasonal home in nearby Paint Bank, Virginia, had concelebrated the August 15 Mass. He then arranged for John Anthony's burial in the small "New Catholic Cemetery" behind the church. Coralie Lewis had started this cemetery in the mid-1940s, presumably because burials there would be easier than going up the hill behind the mansion. The Knights of Columbus supervise the mowing around the church and cemetery, even though the church is closed for most events.[14]

This new development of the use of the little cemetery behind the chapel reminds us of the list of the many buried in the two older cemeteries, who are not directly related to the Floyd and Lewis families.[15] Although direct touch with them has declined sharply with the neglect of those cemeteries, the internet today would permit researchers to reestablish contact. The same would apply to the direct descendants who came from Smithfield and elsewhere for the August 15, 1990, dedication of Letitia Preston Floyd's marker.[16]

Perhaps the brightest hope for a revival of the importance of the Floyd and Lewis families is the renovation of Lynnside and its outbuildings by the current owner. Before the Mass on August 15, 2018, the owner arranged for his manager to guide four of us, Jim Glanville, two Catholics of the parish, and myself, to the root cellar and three other buildings that he has restored. The property is not open to the public, and permission must be obtained.

The owner informed Glanville that he had carefully used wood from nearby Peters Mountain, to preserve the integrity of those buildings. His applications for grants for the renovation of the manor as a national historic site are proceeding as of this printing in 2021.[18]

Despite the the pandemic caused by the Covid-19 corona virus, the Knights of Columbus arranged for Mass to celebrated at St. John's Chapel on August 15, 2020. Thirty-five people were able to fit inside the chapel, observing the pandemic-required social distancing guidelines. A special handout for the Mass memorialized Jim Glanville.[19]

In the mid-1980s, the State of West Virginia surveyed the graves of all past governors for inclusion in the National Register of Historic Places. This resulted in a visit on November 19, 1984, to the Lewis Family Cemetery by Michael Pauley and Daniel Hart of the firm Hart and Pauley, Historic Architectural Surveying and Certification. Lynn Spellman and I showed them St. John's Chapel. They asked that the diocese include the chapel in an expanded Sweet Springs National Register (the Sweet Spring Resort had already been included), and the diocese agreed. They also asked that the derelict mansion be included, and it was.[20]

Pauley concluded in 1991 that this branch of the Floyd Family (the governor and his children) "has remained powerful in Democratic Party politics in southwestern West Virginia until the present time."[21]

Shortly after the process was completed, Spellman told me of a request from the Old Rehoboth Methodist complex that she open the chapel and the three cattle gates to the cemeteries, so a group

At the root cellar of Lynnside. Left to right: Paul Carter, manager of the Lynnside properties; Fr. Harry Winter, O.M.I.; Walter Crone and Hank Richter, Catholic laymen. *Photo by Jim Glanville.*[17]

of historically-minded people could visit the Methodist site in the morning and the Sweet Springs site in the afternoon. She described the visit as a success and a harbinger of future visits.

With the new owner's determination to restore the mansion, even more pieces are now in place for the Floyd and Lewis heritage to be recovered and increased.

Historic marker in Sweet Springs

Woody Holton's book on Abigail Adams reminds us of the exceptional feminist leadership provided by President John Adam's wife.[22] Letitia's letters certainly rival those of Abigail Adams. Glanville was unable to find her original letters to Bishop Whelan, despite the skill he had researching the internet. He and Ryan Mays pointed out "a dramatic growth in the availability of archival records via direct online access," mentioning at least nine new online resources in Virginia, and one in North Carolina for Letitia Preston Floyd alone.[23] When one considers the places where all of the children had lived, the increase of sources of possible material is more than dramatic.

John and Abigail Adams named their only daughter Abigail. John and Letitia Floyd named the eldest of their four daughters Letitia. It can be argued that Letitia Floyd Lewis, by her influence with both Southerners and Northerners at the Sweet Springs Resort, had a greater influence on our country than did Abigail Adams Smith.

Americans from north of the Mason-Dixon line tend to forget the impact of Virginia on our early country. Its geographical size alone is more than Massachusetts. John Adams was a one-term president, as was his son John Quincy Adams. John Floyd was a two-term governor, influential enough to win electoral votes for president in the 1832 election. His son John Buchanan Floyd was governor of Virginia, and the U.S. Secretary of War. Another son, Benjamin Rush Floyd, helped establish freedom of religion when he ran for office. His son George Rogers Clarke Floyd served as Secretary of the Wisconsin Territory before becoming a praised legislator in the State of West Virginia.

Now that the ledgers of the Sweet Springs Resort have become available, it may be possible to see how often Floyd's sons and daughters gathered at their sister Letitia's mansion or at the resort itself during the summer season. I suspect they influenced many during those summers.

Floyd's two other daughters both married influential leaders. When we find the letters of all these children, we will most likely see their importance increase. Perhaps we can look forward to a reevaluation of the Floyd Family, one that compares it favorably with the Adams Family. It is possible that the acclaimed PBS mini-series The Adams Chronicles from 1976 will be paralleled by one called "The Floyd Chronicles." It may be that the current owner's renovation of the Sweet Springs mansion will bring as many people there as now visit Adams' home in Quincy, Massachusetts.

Would the new owner of the resort and the new owner of the mansion work together to make the last week of August and the first week of September again a time for visitors to come to Sweet Springs? Descendants of the Floyd and Lewis families might fill up Sweet Springs by themselves. Perhaps a full scale reenactment of the Union military occupation would be too much for the area, but maybe a partial one could bring in many people.

Ashby Berkley purchased the resort in 2015. He is proposing it become the Sweet Springs Resort Park, "an operating Business and Conference Center, Spa, Recreational Facility, and Public Park for all to enjoy for posterity."[24]

When I concluded my remarks in St. John's Chapel on August 15, 1990, as Bishop Schmitt prepared to bless the marker over Letitia's grave, I quoted an anonymous author who wondered if someday instead of calling Letitia the Abigail Adams of Virginia, we might be calling Abigail the Letitia Floyd of Massachusetts. As usual, the astute Dr. Glanville picked up on the line and realized I was quoting myself.[25]

Another hope for the promotion of the influence of the Floyd and Lewis families is the author, interviewer, and playwright

The Grand Hotel at "Old Sweet," the Sweet Springs Resort,
with its atmosphere of Jeffersonian charm.
used with permission of Mary Katherine Williams

Mary Katherine Williams. Professionally based in Richmond, Virginia, Williams has a seasonal home in Paint Bank, Virginia, just across the state line from Sweet Springs. Among her plays, her stage adaptation of Myles Connolly's classic Catholic novel *Mr. Blue* is the best known.[26] Williams has indicated a "hope to memorialize Letitia Preston Floyd in the form of a poem for an upcoming collection of poems."[27]

Recently, one of the main genealogical websites noted that the three daughters, Letitia Floyd Lewis, Nicketti Floyd Johnston, and Eliza Lavalette Floyd, "all built chapels on their estates in Tazewell and Monroe Counties, which became centers of Catholic activity in the region."[28]

May this be just the beginning of renewed interest in the importance of the Floyd and Lewis families not only on Catholicism, but on the growth of freedom of religion and democracy in our entire country.

CHAPTER EIGHT ENDNOTES

1. David J. Endres, "Dan Lord, Hollywood Priest," *America*, December 12, 2005, 20-21,

2. Harry Winter to Joseph T. McGloin, S.J., April 8, 1989; McGloin to Harry Winter, April 13 and June 6, 1989.

3. Miriam deOlloqui to Harry Winter, undated letter from the 1980s; email from Mimi deOlloqui-Turner and Mimsie deOlloqui, September 8, 2009.

4. Program for Bishop Schulte Taking Possession, October 4, 1986, St. John's folder.

5. Program for April 30, 1988 Confirmation, St. John's folder.

6. The state newspapers reported extensively: *The Monroe Watchman*, November 30, 1989, 12; *The Charleston Gazette*, November 18, 1989, 6A. See the 14-page program for the ordination, prepared by the diocese. Knight of Columbus Mike Williams added to the St. John's Catholic Chapel booklet sometime after 1992, that for the Quincentennial of Columbus' arrival in America, Fr. That-Son returned to the chapel to preside at the Mass.

7. John W. Miller, "Waiting for Morning in Moundsville," *America*, February 19, 2018, 20-25.

8. For the story of the Oblate decline, see Bill O'Donnell, O.M.I., and Harry Winter, O.M.I., "Appalachia, Rise and Fall of Oblate Ministry, 1941-2007," omiusa.org. Also Harry Winter, "Priestless County Adapts," archive page, harrywinter.org.

9. Sr. Molly Bauer, CSJ, to Fr. Harry Winter, O.M.I., April 15, 1994, St. Andrew folder.

10. Warren D. Smith, who did have some overnight guests. He died in 2010. See Mary Katherine Williams, *Sweet Springs: Travel Guide and History*, 52-57 for much on Smith.

11. See the story and photos in the diocesan newspaper *The Catholic Spirit*, September 2, 1988, 3, and omiusa.org, Harry Winter, *Return to Appalachia*, August 15, 2014, 2016, and 2018.

12. Harry Winter, *St. John's Catholic Chapel*, taken over by the Knights of Columbus, Mike Williams, "Tidbits in the History," Spring 1986, available on lynnside.org.

13. R.R. Reno, "While We're At It," *First Things* 256 (October 2015) 68 quoting an obituary in *The Virginian Review*, no date given. The family came again on August 15, 2018, and Msgr. Williams blessed the marker for John. A second infant, Samuel Ignatius Decker, and two other Decker babies (one girl and one boy) are also buried.

14. This cemetery has also been called the "Murphy-Callaghan Cemetery," although that name is in disuse.

15. Robert Neligan arranged for a plaque of his family to be placed on the stairs to the choir loft (dedicated August 15, 2001); several other families are also available in the Cemetery Folder.

16. See Smithfield File, August 15, 1990.

17. Harry Winter, "Return to Appalachia, #3, August 15, 2018," omiusa.org. Paul Carter, the manager; Walter Crone and Hank Richter, the parishioners. Note the second photo, of the inside of the root cellar. Compare the August 15, 2018, photos with the one taken by Lynn Spellman before the renovation: Mary Katherine Williams, *Sweet Springs: Travel Guide and History*, 24.

18. New owner to Glanville, May 21, 2018; July 13, 2018.

19. Mike Williams to Harry Winter, email August 15, 2020.

20. For Michael Pauley's 23-page National Register of Historic Places Form, see lynnside.org, external links.

21. Ibid, Part 8.a.

22. Woody Holton, *Abigail Adams* (New York: Simon & Schuster, 2010).

23. Jim Glanville and Ryan Mays, "A Sketch of Letitia Preston Floyd and Some of Her Letters," *The Smithfield Review (SR)* 19 (2015) 110 (109-11), added to by both, "Letitia Preston Floyd: Supplementary Notes, *SR* 20 (2016) 75. Both available on holstonia.net.

24. The quote is from the website for the Sweet Springs Resort Park, www.sweetspringsresortpark.org; see also website Appalachian Chronicle appalachianchronicle.com, both accessed March 22, 2021.

25. Glanville, SR 19 143, 145. For the sense in which she is an "Oblate Missiologist," see harrywinter.org, Oblate Missiologist page.

26. See Anton J. Pelowski, "Remembering Mr. Blue," Columbia, online edition, June 1, 2014; Mary Katherine Williams, "Letter to the Editor," America, December 19, 2016. Her book *Sweet Springs: Travel Guide and History* cited often above is invaluable.

27. Mary Katherine Williams to Harry Winter, email August. 18, 2018.

28. geni.com/people/Letitia-Lewis search for Letitia Preston Lewis (Floyd) 1814-87, accessed March 2, 2021.

Fr. Harry E. Winter, O.M.I., Ph.D.

Institutional Affiliation / Position: Harry E. Winter is a Missionary Oblate of Mary Immaculate (O.M.I.), residing at the Immaculate Heart of Mary Residence, Tewksbury, Massachusetts. He serves as Coordinator for Mission, Unity, and Dialogue in the O.M.I. U.S.A. Province.

Website: https://harrywinter.org
Telephone: (978) 352-2024
Mailing Address: Father Harry E. Winter, O.M.I.
Saint Mary Parish, 94 Andover Street
Georgetown, MA 01833
E-Mail Address: hewomi@aol.com